LEVEL I
COACHES MANUAL

By: Canadian Coaches

Editors: Claude Lapré
                Keith Wasylik

CANADIAN VOLLEYBALL ASSOCIATION
333 River Road, Vanier, Ontario
CANADA, K1L 8H9

First Printing - April 1986

ISBN 0-920412-54-8

Printed in Canada

ACKNOWLEDGEMENTS

The Canadian Volleyball Association would like to express its thanks to all who contributed to this manual.

The contributing writers:

Charles Cardinal
Professor, Université de Montréal

Brad Kilb
Coach, University of Calgary

Claude Lapré
Technical Coordinator, Canadian Volleyball Association

Guntis Obrascovs
Athletic Therapist, University of Ottawa

Claude Pelletier
Technical Director, Fédération de Volley-Ball du Quebec

Larry Plennart
Former National Team Player
Former Coach, University of Saskatchewan

Lorne Sawula
Head Coach, National Women's Team

Keith Wasylik
Technical Director, Ontario Volleyball Association

The Regional Coaching Chairpersons and the Coaching Development Committee for their leadership and guidance: Charles Cardinal, John Neilson, and Jim Sexsmith.

Sport Canada and the Coaching Association of Canada for providing the means to realize this project.

The Technical Translation Program of the National Sport and Recreation Centre.

Special thanks to the Ontario Volleyball Association and the Fédération de Volley-Ball du Québec for their collaboration and to Lynda Becker and Susan Craig from CVA for their outstanding personal efforts.

PREFACE

"Qui a cessé d'apprendre
doit cesser d'enseigner"

"Coaches Manual Level I" is for all resource persons responsible for a group of participants involved in learning the fundamentals of the game of volleyball. Its main characteristics are basic skill acquisition and elementary team tactics. Also in order to conduct and evaluate adequately their practice session, the coach requires sound pedagogical and training principles. These major tasks are culminated by introducing the players to competition.

The authors of "Coaches Manual Level I" have an extensive volleyball experience as well as technical and pedagogical expertise in our field. We are very grateful that they have accepted to share their knowledge with us. We feel very strongly that the content of the manual will be a useful tool with coaches involved with beginners.

Charles Cardinal
Chairperson
Coaching Development Committee

EDITOR'S NOTE

The purpose of this Manual is to help the candidate in the pursuit of Level I goals. The Manual's contents will, therefore, be closely related to the information necessary to fulfill these objectives.

The main objective of Level I being "to introduce the candidate to the fundamental concepts" of volleyball, the information will be geared to coaching beginners.

The articles related to skills will respect this concept and be limited to the description of basic principles, presentation of a teaching progression for beginners, major faults-errors-corrections and a few simple drills.

The articles related to theoretical knowledge will establish common concepts in training for volleyball. Although our focus is the practice session, the information should provide a logical basis from which we can progress together through CVA's Level I, II and III Technical Clinics and Manuals.

The Level I Manual will be the cornerstone of your future involvement in the Certification Program.

OVERVIEW

Canada's National Coaching Certification Program is designed to meet the needs of practicing coaches, male and female, whether they be beginner or experienced. The program is structured on five levels and presents coaches with the Theoretical, Technical and Practical aspects of coaching.

	Theory	Technical	Practical	Certified
Level One	√	√	√	C
Level Two				
Level Three				
Level Four				
Level Five				

National Coaching Certification Program

1 2 3 4 5

Each coach should participate in all components of the program to develop his/her full potential as a coach. The Theory courses are sponsored by the provincial/territorial governments across the country and relate detailed information on such topics as leadership, motivation, training and teaching methods, etc., common to coaches in all sports. The Technical courses are offered by the national/provincial (territorial) sport associations and present the specific skills, drills, tactics of a particular sport in a progressive, logical sequence. The Practical component of the program consists of actual on-the-field coaching where the principles learned in Theory and Technical are practically applied by coaches working with their athletes. When a coach completes all three components of a level, that coach becomes formally certified and receives a national passport booklet.

Therefore, for coaches who want to avail themselves of all aspects of coaching, opportunities are available through the Theory, Technical and Practical components of Canada's National Coaching Certification Program.

This manual has been produced with the co-operation and financial assistance of the Coaching Association of Canada and Fitness and Amateur Sport, Government of Canada.

The National Coaching Certification Program is developed and implemented through the combined efforts of the Federal Provincial (Territorial) Governments, the National/Provincial (Territorial) Sport Governing Bodies and the Coaching Association of Canada.

Level	Responsibility for Implementation	Major Focus		Theory (hrs. min.)	VOLLEYBALL Technical (hrs. Min.)	Practical (after clinic) (hrs. min.)
I	Provincial/Territorial Governments	Fundamentals -	Daily Practice/ Instruction	14	15	40 hrs.
II	Provincial/Territorial Sport Governing Bodies	and -	Seasonal Schedule	21	27	80 hrs.
III		Development -	Year-round Schedule	30	45	2 years/ 160 hrs.
IV	Federal Government National Sport Governing Bodies and the C.A.C.	National/ International Performance	National Multi-Seasonal Planning	*	100	2 years
V		Elite Player Development	- International	*	*	2 years

(left side label: THEORY / TECHNICAL & PRACTICAL)

* As established by the candidate's learning program.

TABLE OF CONTENTS

CHAPTER 5: **THE FOREARM PASS** *Saturday #1*
By Keith Wasylik

CHAPTER 6: **THE OVERHAND PASS** *Saturday #2*
By Brad Kilb and Keith Wasylik

CHAPTER 7: **THE ATTACK** *Saturday #4*
By Larry Plennart and Keith Wasylik

CHAPTER 8: **THE BLOCK** *Saturday #6*
By Brad Kilb and Keith Wasylik

CHAPTER 14: VOLLEYBALL ADMINISTRATIVE STRUCTURES
By Claude Lapré and Lorne Sawula *Saturday #114*

LEVEL I TO V OBJECTIVES

The objectives of Level I to V Technical and Practical as stated in the CVA Coaching Certification Syllabus are:

Level I: To introduce the candidate to the fundamental concepts of the game of volleyball and planning and conducting principles which will be used in training sessions.

Level II: To provide the candidate with basic Technical and Tactical knowledge of the game in a manner which will enable the candidate to apply this knowledge in the following situations:

- Planning seasonal training
- Conducting a team in competition
- Evaluation of the athlete and the team

Level III: To prepare the coach to train a team towards a volleyball performance. Two major components will be dealt with: ability to coach and knowledge.

Level IV: To lead the coach through an intense experience which will enhance his/her comprehension on the attitudes, knowledge and abilities required to raise the performance of the team at the national level.

Level V: To adequately prepare our elite coaches to compete at the international level. Level V is a tutorship program. Every candidate's program will be tailored to suit his needs and reach specific objectives.

LEVEL I TECHNICAL

As for Level I Technical, the specific objectives, criteria for candidacy and criteria for achievement are as follows:

OBJECTIVES

KNOWLEDGE OBJECTIVES

- Knowledge of the basic skills required to play the game
- Knowledge of standard situations and team formations for beginners
- Knowledge on the players technical evolution
- Knowledge on common faults and errors and how to detect and correct them
- Knowledge on planning a training session
- Knowledge on how to select drills favoring motor skills acquisition
- Knowledge on how to conduct a training session:
  EXPLANATION - DEMONSTRATION - FEEDBACK
- Knowledge of basic rules and regulations

ABILITY OBJECTIVES

- To be able to perform basic coach ball handling skills

CRITERIA FOR CANDIDACY

Being actively involved in volleyball as a player, or a teacher, or an instructor, or an official, or a coach, or as a student.

CRITERIA FOR ACHIEVEMENT

- 100% attendance and participation at a Level I clinic

LEGEND

These symbols will be used throughout the manual.

Net	○————————○
Orientation of the player on the court	⊔
Player blocking	⊓
Player holding ball	⊔•
Player identified by his/her jersey number	⌊12⌋ ⌊3⌋
Player identified by his/her position on the court	① ③
Path of moving player	– – – – – →
Path of moving ball	————→
Path of ball after attack	═══════➤
Setter	S
Coach	△
Shagger	•
Feeder	▪
Target	●
Ball Bucket	⊡
Table	☐
Obstacle	●
Wall	⌈⊤⊤⊤⊤⊤⊤⊤⊤⌉

EXAMPLES

Diagram 1

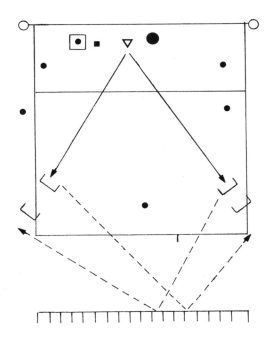

Diagram 2

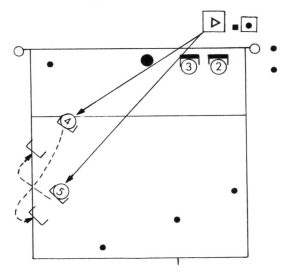

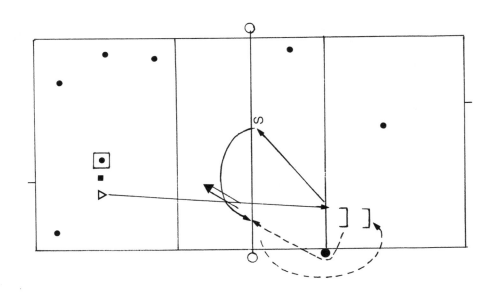

TECHNICAL DEVELOPMENT OF
THE VOLLEYBALL PLAYER

By Charles H. Cardinal

TECHNICAL DEVELOPMENT
OF THE
VOLLEYBALL PLAYER

The Coach's main role will be to pursue the technical development of his players. This role requires an analytical, systematic approach if we want to reach optimal efficiency.

Upon completion of this unit, the coach will have a better understanding of the following:

- the stages of technical development of a volleyball player

- the tasks and requirements of each stage

- the role of the coach at each stage

The technical efficiency of an athlete during competition is comparable to that of a musician or a craftsman. The dexterity acquired after long hours of work is used to create a piece of work in a momentary performance. Technical efficiency can be defined as doing the right movement for a specific situation at a given time. It becomes evident that the sought-after perfection of these gestures is a long term process requiring a large number of correct repetitions carried out under conditions created by a coach. Efficiency of technical movements in competition is then a variable factor which affects performance. Attainment of this technical efficiency by an athlete is influenced by a coach.

In our opinion, it is essential that "a coach consider his role as helping an athlete to develop as harmoniously as possible and to realize his potential by helping him/her to overcome increasingly complex situations adapted to his capacities" (H.C.J.L.S., 1978). The pursuit of this objective is based on the respect and application of the following main principles:

- The technical development of the athlete must be considered as a comprehensive, progressive and continuous entity

- The skill training and optimal development of physical qualities required for the activity, are closely related and will condition and influence each other

- The use of a theoretical model comprised of the elements to be mastered by an athlete at each stage of his evolution

This article is limited to the steps to be completed in the technical development of a volleyball player, the conditions to be set out by a coach and the objectives pursued:

- Teaching the mechanics of a movement
- Familiarization with a movement
- Developing tactical intelligence
- Integrating the player/skill into a system of play
- Verifying the efficiency of a player/skill through competition

A coach looks for results of technical efficiency, that is, ability to hold up in competition. To do this, his plan for development must include the following components:

- The level of formation reached by the participant in the activity
- The physical and motor abilities of the participant
- Psychological factors and individual objectives (desire to work, desire to improve, need for self-realization, etc.)

From an athlete's point of view, his/her reward and motivation come from the fact that through training and coaching, he/she is able to do today what was impossible yesterday.

TEACHING THE MECHANICS
OF A MOVEMENT

At the start of technical training, no matter the method, an athlete must imitate a model as closely as possible. This model is usually a coach (or a successful athlete) who demonstrates the proper execution of a technique. To reproduce the model exactly, an athlete must have an accurate mental image of the movement. Audio-visual methods can help in this regard. A series of successive photos illustrating the execution of the movement, a film, observation of successful athletes in competition are current methods to be used by a coach. It is, however, important to emphasize that the attention of athletes be kept only on elements essential to this stage. Technical details are presented later, after the athlete has completed the exercise with a success rate of 70% or more. We thus see a systematic evolution where the main thrust of the exercise switches from a particular segment or part of the movement, to a complete execution of the movement. An understanding of physical laws and mechanical principles governing body movement is vital to efficient teaching. This approach allows a coach to decide what is right, possible, important, and what is not. Furthermore, the attention of a coach is centered on the causes of errors and interventions favouring improvement in the efficiency of a movement.

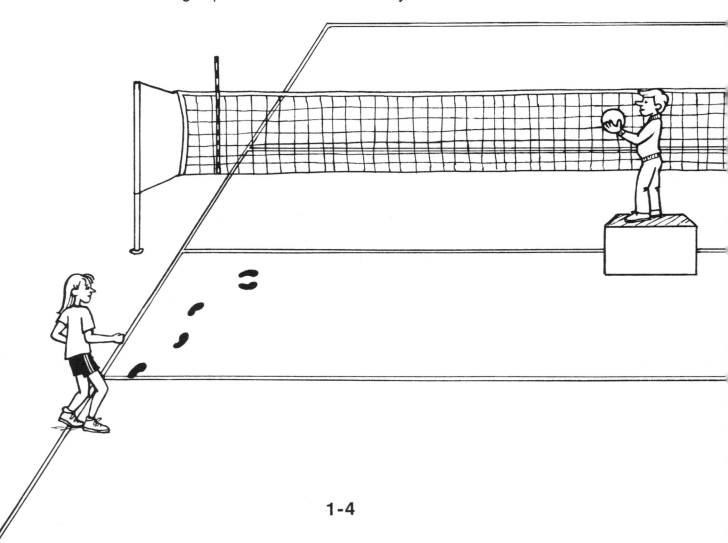

An athlete is first placed under artificial conditions and then under easy and constant conditions. Working conditions are completely isolated from the reality of a match. Firstly, the coach uses visual aids, auxiliary materials and appropriate equipment to help in the acquisition of the motor skill. For example, drawing footwork for the approach and the take-off point for the spike; using balls of various weights and sizes to introduce contact with the ball, etc. Secondly, give the athlete simple exercises geared at overcoming internal constraints, only, this means complete respect of basic principles in positioning, direction of movement, dynamics and timing of the movement, the sequential use of segments, etc., in order to have a proper feeling for the exact movement. The objective is to progressively acquire the global motor skill involved.

It is very important for a coach to increase the volume of training, that is the frequency and length of the actions. Do not forget that practice, or repetition, generates habits. However, if you are not insistent and the young person practices any way he/she feels like, problems may result. It is not enough to maintain that training be done a certain number of hours per week. A coach must ensure that the exercises are properly executed if he/she wants to develop habits which will allow the attainment of technical efficiency.

FAMILIARIZATION
WITH A MOVEMENT

At this stage, the requirements of the task come closer to the actual conditions for execution. All artificial conditions are then eliminated. A coach progressively increases the' requirements of an athlete, while continuing to maintain a high level of quality as far as execution of the technique is concerned. To do this, new requirements cannot be introduced until the athlete sufficiently masters those from the previous stage. On the other hand, if the requirements put on an athlete are too easy for his/her level, the exercises will not stimulate him/her thus holding up his/her development and progress.

Following are the different variables which can be manipulated by a coach:

- Increasing physical requirements by increasing:
  - speed of execution of the movement
  - strength of application or resistance
  - distance to be covered for a given time
  - the height or length to be attained
  - and by playing with intensity and recovery time

- Calling for accuracy of a movement and consistency in performance: It is not sufficient at this stage to just return the ball to a partner; it must also be returned accurately. Furthermore, an athlete must be able to repeat the movement regularly and efficiently, even if the conditions are changing.

- Add before or after performance of the skill, different types of movements, or changes in direction. A coach can also introduce going from one skill to another or changing rhythm of performance of the same motor skill.

- Ensure that the skill is carried out in various locations on the court. Examples: low defence in 1,6, and 5; spikes at the net in 4,3, and 2.

At this stage, familiarization with the movement is done under conditions controlled by the coach. Exercises are various and diverse. Technique will be assimilated as quickly as possible in a systematic but kinetic way, by modifying the conditions for execution. The choice of exercises and their sequential order of presentation must follow a certain progression in terms of difficulty of the task imposed on the athlete, from a perceptual point of view as well as from a motor point of view. In this type of work situation, there is only one response: an athlete does not have many solutions to choose from. He/she knows beforehand the motor task to be accomplished. So, the athlete is the only person involved in the exercise, there is emphasis on only one role, or only one technical element is stressed. If other players and movements are required, they are only auxiliary to the proper performance of the exercise. Exercises used by the coach must respect the following constraints:

- the sequential order of motor skills while playing
- the notion of rhythm in exercise
- spatial orientation of players on the court
- the movements found in a game

Very briefly, the carrying-out of a task at the stage of familiarization with a movement, calls for perceptive-kinetic requirements related to speed of reaction, speed of movement, body precision, and motor accuracy. The participant is preoccupied with assessing the trajectory of the ball, its speed, and its place of landing, and by the nature, direction, and accuracy of the return by choosing the proper technical response, respecting the rules of play. The objective at this stage is twofold. Firstly, there is development of specific details of skills for competition (example: footwork and positioning, or the movement of the attacking arm, etc.). Secondly, the technique becomes consolidated and stable so that a player can bring his/her selective attention to more complex tactical tasks.

During competition, situations change quickly. A tactical problem can and must be resolved through various techniques. A player who always uses the same skill becomes stereotyped, making it easier for the opposition. However, it is hardly possible that all motor skills used in volleyball be consolidated and stable. This is why only basic motor skills are stabilized. As soon as an athlete has fairly mastered the basic motor skills, a coach can introduce variations to these movements thus increasing his repertory of tactical solutions.

DEVELOPING TACTICAL
INTELLIGENCE

The behaviour of a highly skilled player shows efficient application of successive skills. "This application of successive skills is the basis of team play" (Mahlo, 1969). This succession of movements in a game is the individual response of an athlete to a problem confronting him/her in a given situation. If a player does not need to focus attention and intellectual ability on the performance of these skills, he/she can instead concentrate on the more complicated tactical tasks. "These combinations of movements will then be guided by kinesthetic sensations and by perception" (Cardinal, Boulonne, Caron, 1975).

It then becomes vital at this stage of an athlete's evolution to be able to retain pertinent information on various playing situations so he/she can act in time, and not react to a situation, or to the ball. Each playing situation creates a problem, a tactical problem for the team and more particularily for the player called on to play the ball. Thus, a playing situation is the result of an action with the ball, and the motor response of the player at this particular moment to solve a temporary tactical problem will create a new series, a succession of different and changing playing situations, which materialize through direct actions with the ball (Baacke, 1978).

It is a coach's role to bridge the skill to other related motor skills, and to introduce its proper application in multiple playing situations. "All motor behaviour, such as that which appears in sports in the form of relatively complicated movements, presupposes programmed skills" (Schnabel, 1968). Therefore, during a game, programming of proper motor responses meets the requirements of a situation based on the gathering of pertinent information. This information comes from the following sources:

- direction, trajectory, speed, and landing spot of the ball
- position and play actions of partners
- position and play actions of opponents
- external conditions such as: score, refereeing, rhythm and momentum of the game, lighting, space around the court, height of the ceiling, spectators, etc.
- the tactical intention of the player playing the ball, that is the return of the ball

A player in a playing situation must not only see a lot of things, but must also, with complete perception, pick out the essential and isolate the unessential in the shortest time possible. "In all team sports, the motor response must be adapted to what is happening during play thus giving extreme importance to perception of requirements of the situation" (Thiffault, 1975).

Conditions created by the coach for application of skills must be similar or identical to the competition conditions, that is: speed of execution, rhythm, spatio-temporal orientation, relationship with partners, knowledge of opponents. Under competitive conditions, several players are involved, with assigned tactical tasks. Cooperation, synchronization and complicity between players are essential to resolve the task. These conditions call for an athlete to make a quick analysis of the situation and a decision based on a choice of methods, according to both partners and opponents.

By creating actual game conditions in training, a coach can manipulate one or several of the following variables. First, include the skill in a succession of motor skills. Second, increase the difficulty of the task by properly manipulating the intensity of the exercise, the recovery period, length of the exercise, and frequency. Third, increase the complexity of the task so the player has to think about the situation and choose the proper response from several alternatives. It is then important to make the player competent at choosing the best solution, from several possibilities, for a given momentary situation.

At this stage of a player's development, a coach pursues several objectives. A player must become progressively autonomous in the organization on the court. He/she must be able to complete a task will less effort. His behaviour must reflect progressive control of uncertainty. And finally, he/she must aim for increased efficiency in information gathering. Exercises chosen by a coach must allow players to reach these objectives. A player must be able to evaluate his own tactical behaviour in order to efficiently adapt himself to changing situations.

INTEGRATING A PLAYER/ SKILL INTO A SYSTEM OF PLAY

According to Théodorescu (1965), a system of play can be defined as follows: "a general way of organizing offensive or defensive actions of players by stabilizing a precise plan for certain tasks - by positions and sections - as well as certain principles of cooperation among them." At this stage of a player's development, one of the coach's goals should be the methodical development of actions (technical-tactical movement) and of tactical thought. As tactics largely depend on intellectual standards, it appears necessary that an athlete reach the following objectives within a training situation which almost totally respect the conditions found in competition.

To increase tactical knowledge, to reinforce it, systemize it, with the intention of rapid actualization in concrete situations: this is the learning process of the role and responsibilities of a player during various moments of a game. A film of a match will show, for attack as well as for defense, moments of play clearly defined in time and place and, according to the rules of the game, the different possibilities (motor response) offered to a player. Each moment of the game is characterized by a tactical task subject to the activity of each player and those of the entire team. "Without common awareness of concrete realities and without harmonious tactical knowledge, the potential unity of play favourable to a team is not possible" (Rioux et Chappuis, 1967).

To develop a system of associative solutions: This method is considered the quickest way of linking perception to a tactical solution. "If all team members have identical training, there is homogeneous perception of the structure of the action and instant comprehension based on the associative solution" (Mahlo, 1969). Associative solutions to simple tactical problems is a feature of a mature player. The ability to establish a mental association between the perceived situation and a corresponding solution, represents the quickest method of mentally solving the problem at the appropriate moment in a game.

To train independent productive thinking: This phase includes the capacity to analyze a situation and to transfer known solutions to new and analogous problems (Mahlo, 1969). The highest form of technical-tactical movement conveys the importance of the intellectual component through tactical awareness, topped with independent productive thinking. It is creative thinking in the sense that new concrete solutions are found and that it is a source of new general knowledge (Mahlo, 1967).

To create a power struggle with the opponent: To disrupt the opponent's trends and strong points and to take advantage of his weaknesses, deficiencies, and inadequacies. This adaptation towards an opponent done during training, is to make a player capable of solving practical problems by himself during a match. However, training alone is not enough to develop tactical thinking. It is during a match, under various stress situations imposed on an athlete, that tactical thinking can reach its height. A coach must be aware that "the quality of perception increases from a tactical point of view at the same time as knowledge, along with the conditioning of the player, his perceptive training" (Cardinal, Boulonne, Caron, 1975). This means that when a player is aware of technical-tactical particularities of opponents, his/her perception and analysis of a playing situation is favourably influenced, facilitating and accelerating the proper response. Thus, tactical knowledge, advance information about what an opponent will do, and experience of players are factors which influence the speed and accuracy with which a player adapts during competition.

The acquisition of efficient tactical thinking makes systematic intervention by a coach indispensable. The framework for an athlete's work, which emerges as a system of play, must take into account the actual characteristics of players. It is dangerous to blindly copy what other teams of high calibre do. Intervention by a coach in this context must be done with the objective of making players capable of thinking about and solving their own problems. A coach must then use different competitive situations such as controlled play and experimental matches where there are certain beneficial features to aid the decision-making of players in resolving tactical problems, while ensuring their autonomy on the court. Realization of the task by a player in a system of play calls for motor, perceptual, and memory requirements.

VERIFYING THE EFFICIENCY OF A PLAYER/SKILL THROUGH COMPETITION

Once an athlete becomes involved in a game, a coach is generally very limited in his interventions. He/she has only two time-outs and six substitutions. He/she has no control of the situation. An athlete alone faces the performance to be carried out; it is he/she who plays. In the midst of action, a player must try to carefully manipulate the following variables: concentration, self-control, correction of movements, and adaptation to situations as they occur.

Of course, these variables must be emphasized in the previous stages if positive results are to be obtained. It is absurd to require disciplined behaviour of your athletes if you only talk about it for the first time during a match. If you have not created conditions appropriate for learning the previously mentioned variables, you might end up with a good technician, a marvelous stylist who will impress spectators during pre-competition warm-up. He/she will not, however, measure up to your expectations under the stress of competition.

CONCLUSION

It seems obvious to us that to attain technical efficiency during competition, a coach cannot limit interventions to helping a player acquire a skill and leave the rest to chance. He/she is responsible for gradually and progressively bringing an athlete over increasing difficulties up to the efficient application of skills during competition. However, it is necessary to differentiate between efficiency which means a job well done, one which is technically correct, and effectiveness which means doing well what one is supposed to do; in other words, using the proper skill for the situation at hand. To reach this objective, a coach must ensure he/she creates learning conditions which favour execution of dynamic and flexible motor stereotypes.

SUMMARY

- The steps of technical development can be identified as:

    - teaching the mechanics of a movement

    - familiarization with a movement

    - developing tactical intelligence

    - integrating the player/skill into a system of play

    - verifying the efficiency of a player/skill through competition

- The development process is geared towards correct and appropriate use of skills in competition.

- The technical development is closely related to the development of physical qualities.

- The technical and tactical development must be considered as an entity.

BIBLIOGRAPHY

Cardinal, C.H.,   Boulonne, G.C., Caron, J.H. L'acte tactique et sa préparation. La préparation d'un champion. Québec: Editions du Pélican, 1975.

Cardinal, C.H.   Notes de cours. D.H.F.K. Leipzig: R.D.A., 1978.

Mahlo, F.   L'acte tactique en jeu. Belgique, 1969.

H.C.J.L.S.   Rapport du comité d'étude sur la formation des cadres sportifs québécois. Québec: H.C.J.L.S., 1978.

Rious, G., Chappuis, R.   L'équipe dans les sports collectifs. Paris: 1967

Schnabel, G.   La coordination des gestes. Wissensschaff Liche Zeitschrift der D.H.F.K. R.D.A.: 1968.

Theorodescu, L.   Principes pour l'étude tactique commune aux jeux sportifs collectifs et leur corrélation avec la préparation tactique des équipes et des joueurs. E.P.S., avril-mai, 1965.

Thiffault, C.   Efficacité technique du joueur d'avant au hockey sur glace. Mouvement. Spécial hockey 2. Montréal: avril 1965.

CHOICE AND STRUCTURE

OF DRILLS

By Claude Pelletier

CHOICE AND STRUCTURE
OF DRILLS

One of the main tasks of the coach is to find a means of developing the physical, technical and tactical qualities of his/her athlete(s). To do this, the coach must choose, and even develop, drills consistent with the objective and practice themes of the training session.

Upon completion of this unit, the coach should have a better understanding of:

-   the broad and specific classification of drills

-   the relation between the categories of drills and the task to be accomplished

-   how to build drills to meet the team's needs

One of the difficulties young coaches have is the preparation of appropriate drills. Most take their drills directly from manuals and make no attempt to adapt them to their clientèle. It is, therefore, important for a young coach to be able to develop his/her own drills consistent with the needs of his/her athletes.

This ability to choose and/or develop drills is not easily acquired. Experience and, above all, better manipulation of the different variables used to develop drills, will make him/her a more competent coach as far as the preparation of his/her training sessions and fulfillment of his/her tasks are concerned.

CLASSIFICATION OF DRILLS

There are, depending on the author, a number of ways to classify drills. The most common used in sports terminology is the division of drills into three broad classifications: general drills, specific drills, and competition drills.

GENERAL DRILLS

° Definition:	These are drills derived from other sports.
° Characteristics:	No similarity with the movement used specifically in competition. They only indirectly influence the development of performance factors used specifically in competition.
° Goals:	- Overall physical preparation - To prevent boredom and saturation - Active recreation - To offset intensive training
° Methods:	- Gymnastic exercises with or without the use of a ball. - Exercises on gym apparatus - Running, cross-country skiing, cycling, etc.

SPECIFIC DRILLS

° Definition:	The executed move contains elements of a competition movement, with quite a number of the muscles working in a similar, or in the same way as they would when executing the movement in competition.

º Characteristics:	The coach places the athlete in various controlled conditions that are perfectly, or almost perfectly, consistent with the direction and the dynamic and temporal progression of the movement.
º Goals:	The development of technical or technicotactical details of movements used specifically in competition. The specific and localized development of one or more factors determining athletic performance, that is, specific physical preparation.
º Methods:	- Simple drills - Complex drills - Relays, contests, games

COMPETITION DRILLS

º Definition:	The skill executed by the athlete is consistent with the regulations of his/her discipline.
º Characteristics:	The conditions in which the movement is executed perfectly, or almost perfectly, duplicate the conditions encountered in competition with respect to movement sequence, speed of execution, rhythm, synchronization, coordination, etc.
º Goals:	The proper and complex development of movement executions used specifically in competition.
º Methods:	- Match - Controlled play - Modified 2 vs 2, 3 vs 3 play

CATEGORIES OF DRILLS

Based on this very broad classification and taking somewhat greater account of the characteristics of team sports, the drills can be more precisely defined by subdividing them into seven categories:

º Simple drills
º Combined drills
º Drills of simple action sequences
º Complex drills
º Drills of complex action sequences
º Formation drills
º Game drills

SIMPLE DRILLS

The simple drill develops motor skills and generally covers just one technical element. The athlete is placed in artificial conditions designed to promote the acquisition of motor skills. He/she may also be placed in simple and constant conditions to promote the acquisition, automation, consolidation and stabilization of the skill.

The player must focus his/her attention on the technical elements of the movement. He/she may act alone with the ball or react to a ball tossed by a teammate or by the coach (see Figure 1, 2 and 3).

Example 1:

Figure 1

Example 2:

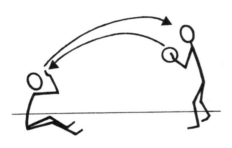

Figure 2

Example 3:

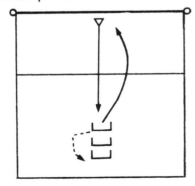

Figure 3

Alone with the ball

- hits ball against the wall (attack motion)

- elements to concentrate on - ball contact and height of contact

2 players, 1 ball

- arm movement on ball contact

- the ball is tossed by a teammate at chest level

- contact by the seated player, who must return the ball with an overhand pass to his/her teammate, who is standing

1 coach, 1 player, 1 ball

- ball contact using forearm pass

- the coach (△) tosses an easy ball to the player in front of him/her, who must return the ball using the forearm pass

- group of 3 - 10 balls per player

As illustrated in the examples, the player is always alone in relation to the ball. The task is simple and the player is always placed in controlled conditions.

Simple drills are used primarily in the stages of discovering the mechanics of the skill and familiarization with the skill. During the drill, the participant is, therefore, subject only to "internal limitations of execution, that is, the correct positioning of the feet, the direction of the movement, the dynamic and temporal progression of the movement, the sequential order of activation of the body segments, in order to gain an accurate sense of the movement" (Cardinal, 1983). The athlete is placed in conditions that are artificial or simple and constant.

COMBINED DRILLS

Combined drills may be used when the participant has a relative mastery of the motor skill(s). The athlete may then be placed in conditions controlled by the coach. Technical performance is the dominant factor in combined drills; a high degree of skill of execution is still called for, while the demands of the drills are increased by relating them more closely to the actual conditions under which they will be performed.

It is important, in combined drills, with regard to the technical development, to follow a certain progression in the requirements and, in particular, to manipulate the following variables:

- ° increase the physical demands,
- ° demand precision of movement and consistency of performance,
- ° precede or follow up the execution of the technical skill with an action, a court movement, and/or some other movement
- ° ensure that the technical movement is executed at various places on the court" (Cardinal, 1983).

Following are several examples to illustrate the manipulation of these variables.

First, using combined drills, the coach must increase the physical demands, by manipulating the variables of volume, intensity, and density. He/she will thus vary the duration, rhythm, ball speed, path of the ball, and intervals of rest according to his/her objectives (see Figure 4).

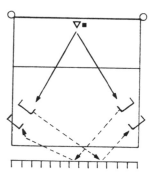

Figure 4

- ° Group of 4 - 20 balls per player: Increased duration (volume).

   OR

- ° Group of 4 - 10 balls per player, but the coach (Δ) accelerates the rhythm of his/her hits, causing the players to move more quickly and thus increasing intensity slightly.

   OR

○ Group of 4 - 10 balls per player; the coach maintains the same hitting rhythm but causes the path of the ball to become increasingly difficult.

Once the athletes are able to perform their technical skills correctly in controlled conditions, the coach can insist on precision and consistency of performance. Now, the athlete must not only play the ball, but he/she must return it to a specific point indicated by the coach. Also, the athlete must achieve a certain consistency in his/her performance, that is, send the ball regularly to a specific point on the court, while correctly executing his/her motor skills (see Figure 5).

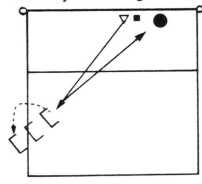

Figure 5

○ Precision:

- Group of 4 - 10 balls per player

- The coach tosses the ball to all players in 5, in consecutive tosses. Once a player has contacted the ball, he/she moves to position 1. When all players are in position 1, the coach tosses the ball to each in turn. The players return the ball to the target (●).

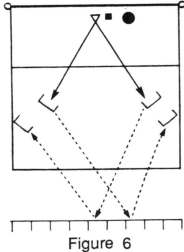

Figure 6

○ After returning the ball with a forearm pass, the player moves quickly to touch the wall and continues on to the other position.

○ Precision and Consistency:

- Same drill structure, but this time the players have completed the drill when they have returned the ball to the target five (5) consecutive times.

Then, while maintaining the physical demands, the coach will ask the athlete to perform a technical skill, having him/her precede or follow it up with a movement or court movement (see Figure 6).

○ Group of 4 - 10 balls per player
○ The drill begins with 2 players at position 5 and 2 others at position 1
○ The coach begins by tossing the ball to position 5, then to position 1, and so on

Finally, the coach should ensure that the athlete is able to execute the skill from various places on the court, while still increasing the physical demands or demands for precision and consistency.

When the athlete is executing a technical skill in a combined drill, it is the role of the coach to ensure, first, that the athlete assumes the correct basic position, moves properly on the court and positions his/her feet correctly, and second, that the athlete correctly executes the skill; that is, his/her observations and intervention should still focus on the elements that revolve around the execution of the skill. "Thus, in the drill, only one athlete is called upon, only one role emphasized, or only one technical element stressed. Any other players and moves required are complementary to the progression of the drill" (Cardinal, 1983).

DRILLS OF SIMPLE ACTION SEQUENCES

Once the athlete has good control of his/her technical moves in controlled conditions, he/she must then be able to combine motor skills sequentially. To practice this, the following method is used: Drills of simple action sequences. This consists in placing the athlete in conditions where he/she must execute two or three actions.

Drills of simple action sequences are used to familiarize the athlete with the skill. During this stage, the drill of simple action sequences is carried out in conditions controlled by the coach, that is, simple and constant conditions. The athlete has no choice of solutions: In performing the skill or skills, he/she knows in advance what motor skill will be required. The coach must, however, observe the following constraints when developing a sequential action drill:

○ "The sequential order of the motor skills in game situation,
○ the notion of rhythm in the drill,
○ the spatial orientation of the player(s) on the court,
○ court movements encountered in a game situation" (Cardinal, 1983).

Let us look at two examples of sequential action drills used at the stage of familiarization with a skill:

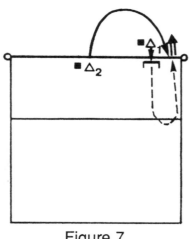

Figure 7

○ counter attack sequences:

- the player begins at the net. The coach hits the ball to his/her hands and he/she blocks it. Then, the player moves back to the attack line to take up a better position for attacking a second ball tossed by the other coach.

Once the athlete is able to perform two actions in sequence in controlled conditions, while executing perfectly his/her two technical skills, the coach can increase the performance demands (see Figure 8).

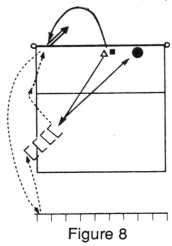

Figure 8

○ Group of 3 - 20 balls per player

○ The coach (△) hits the ball to a defence player, who must return it to the target

○ If he/she does so successfully, he/she moves to position 4 to attack a second ball tossed by the coach

○ Then, he/she moves to touch the wall and returns to position 5.

COMPLEX DRILLS

Complex drills are aimed primarily at coordinating the actions of two or more players to develop their knowledge of, and strengthen their individual tactics specific to each position. These drills must promote the combination of a number of elements of play while respecting the sequential order of a game's progression and calling for the cooperation of a number of players and brainwork to resolve a tactical problem.

In complex drills, the player's intervention is usually limited to an offensive or defensive action in a temporary or partial phase of play. The execution of this movement, however, "calls primarily on perceptual skills related to the discrimination of information, the classification and interpretation of data, for reflection and decision and choice-making" (Cardinal, 1983). This entire process, complex as it is, must be topped off with the proper motor response for solving the problem (see Figure 9).

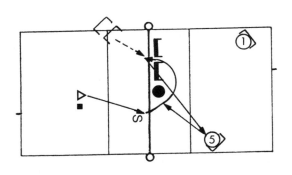

Figure 9

○ The coach (△) throws the ball to the setter (S), who passes to the attacker (⌴), who attacks the ball to the player in position 5 or 1, or tips depending on the quality of the set and the placement of the blockers.

○ The back-court players in positions 1 and 5 must respond properly to the intentions of the attacker and according to the placement of the blockers. The player must recover the ball if it enters his/her zone and return it to position "2 1/2".

Complex drills require the participation of a number of players who are teammates or opponents. The demands are primarily perceptual in the sense that the player must execute the proper action according to the situation he/she encounters. It is at this stage that he/she begins to resort to individual tactics.

In short, complex drills are used primarily when the coach wants to stabilize the skill in difficult and complex conditions. In other words, the conditions of execution "must respect perfectly, or almost perfectly, the situations encountered in competition, that is, speed of execution, rhythm, spatiotemporal orientation, relation with teammates, notion of opponents. A number of players are called on to perform in competitive conditions by being assigned a tactical task. Cooperation, complementarity, complicity among players are essential to accomplishing the task" (Cardinal, 1983).

DRILLS OF COMPLEX ACTION SEQUENCES

During the stage of applying the skill in complex drills, the coach may also use drills of complex action sequences. This type of drill enables the coach to "build a bridge between relative mastery of the technical skill, introduction within a series of motor skills, and proper application in numerous game situations" (Cardinal, 1983). The conditions for performing the skill within the drill are perfectly, or almost perfectly, consistent with situations encountered in competition. That is, the athlete must perform a sequence of actions, while having to analyze the situation and make a decision in the use of the proper skill, taking his/her teammates and his/her opponents into account.

Let us look at a drill of complex action sequences that illustrates this:

- sequence of defence in position 4 and attack in position 4

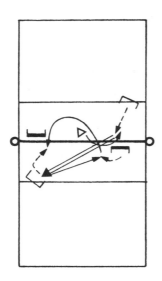

Figure 10

° The coach (△) throws a high ball to position 4 that is attacked into midcourt (aim at the defence player), avoiding the blocker.

° The blocker, having attempted to block the attack, moves to position 3 to set the ball. He/she then becomes a setter.

° The defence player (⊔) in position 4 recovers the attack from the opponent's court, and returns it to the setter.

° The defence player, after his/her recovery, moves to position 4 and attacks the set made by the setter. The attacker must avoid the block and attack along the line or the crosscourt, depending on the position of the blocker in position 2.

FORMATION DRILLS

Formation drills are situations set up by the coach to practice certain phases of the game. These are real game segments in which sequences of actions are built such as serve reception and counter-attack, defence and counter-attack, attack coverage and counter-attack, etc. Using these formation drills, it is possible to incorporate the players into a given system of play and distinct tactical patterns, with a view to implementing the roles of each player (see Figure 11).

- drill for serve reception and the counter-attack:

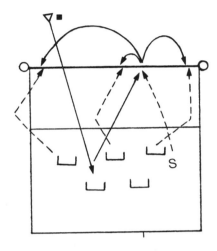

Figure 11

o formation for serve reception with the back row setter (S)

o reception by a player who passes it to the setter, an attack set to position 4, 3 or 2, attack and coverage

o switching of players according to specialization

o rotation after 10 successful attacks

GAME DRILLS

Game drills are drills intended to teach the players to think and solve problems that confront them during play. These drills are types of competition that highlight certain situations that should prompt the players to take decisions as well as to resolve the problems they come up against. Also, these game drills should promote the stabilization and consolidation of technical skills in a game situation.

We can distinguish three types of game drills:

o modified games
o controlled games
o practice games

Modified Games

Modified games are 2 on 2, 3 on 3 play patterns executed on an adapted court according to rules set by the coach. The players are thus called on to play both offence and defence, and to make the transition from one to the other. This last characteristic makes this type of drill more complete than complex drills (see Figure 12).

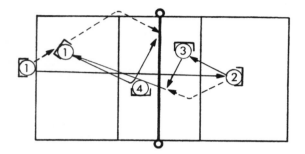

Figure 12

- #1 serves to #2; #2 passes to #3 and moves up to tip/hit to #1. #1 then passes to #4 for set and attack

- 10 successful attacks

- variation: change role with partner after each sequence

Controlled Games

Controlled games consists in presenting a problematic solution in which the players focus on a temporary or partial phase of play. The coach's role is of prime importance in this type of drill. Often, he/she will act directly on the ball to better control the task to be executed. His/her instructional intervention as well as his/her feedback to the players will be of considerable importance in the tactical learning process. The coach should teach the players to identify the problem and analyze with him/her the appropriate solution (see Figure 13).

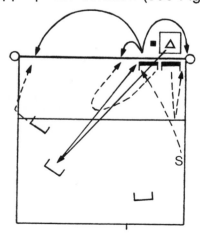

Figure 13

- Defence drill from a position 4 attack

- The coach mounts a table close to the net and attacks the balls to the defence players. He/she analyzes the players' court movements and actions as well as the organization of the counter-attack.

Practice Game

Practice games are a means used by the coach to verify the technical efficiency of the players in a game situation, as well as their cooperation with each other and their attitude. It sometimes is also used to assess the team's preparation for a future performance or to make necessary corrections within a training cycle.

Practice games must be fully and completely consistent with the conditions encountered in competition, even if the games are limited to opposing members of the same team. Winning is not the object of practice games.

Formation drills, modified games, controlled games and practice games are all methods whereby the coach is able to integrate one or more motor skills into a system of play. These categories of drills bring out "certain beneficial characteristics of decision-making on the part of the players in resolving a tactical problem, and stabilize the technicotactical moves in a game situation. The player's performance of the task within the play pattern calls on motor, perceptual and memory skills" (Cardinal, 1983). All of these further the building of a system of "associations-solutions", that is, to create a link as quickly as possible between what is perceived and the representation of a tactical solution.

STRUCTURE OF A DRILL

It is desirable that the coach not use trial and error in the preparation and choice of drills. Now that the coach is aware of the main categories of drills, we wish to make his/her task easier by suggesting a method for developing drills.

OBJECTIVE

The objective is the main element the coach wishes to work on in relation to the tasks to be performed by the athlete. This objective must be clearly identified, specific and attainable, that is, it must be quantifiable and measurable. The objective must be adapted to the level of the players and, above all, it must clearly identify the task to be undertaken. A sample objective is provided in Table 2.

CONTEXT AND CONDITIONS OF EXECUTION

Once the task and objective have been clearly identified, the coach should choose an appropriate drill. He/she should explain the procedure for completing the drill. Following is the information the coach should give the athletes when explaining the task and limitations of the drill:

° number of players
° positioning of the players
° path and circulation of the ball
° court movement of the player(s)
° return point of the ball
° role of the players not involved in the drill
° rhythm, specific load, number of series and repetitions, rest time
° delimitation of the space used
° role of the coach (active, passive) (see Table 2)

DRILL VARIANT

The drill variant(s) consist(s) in specifying the possible modifications within a given drill structure, for various sequences or after a certain time. For example, a coach may repeat the same drill structure two or three times consecutively. He/she will, however, introduce certain variants if he/she wishes to increase or decrease the difficulty or complexity of the task to be worked on (see Table 2).

SUCCESS CRITERION

In each drill, the coach must establish a success criterion to verify whether the objective has been attained. The success criterion may be quantitative (i.e. successful completion of 10 consecutive serves) or qualitative (i.e. return a serve to a specific point or stress the use of the right skill in a given situation). The success criterion will depend on the nature of the drill and the task to be performed.

INDICATORS - REFERENCE POINTS

To give a better idea of what he/she is looking for in a drill and to enable him/her to intervene more effectively, the coach should establish reference points that will help him/her know where to direct his/her attention and intervention with the athlete. These reference points should guide the coach as to the nature of his/her interventions.

EVALUATION

The coach should note whether his/her objective has been reached; if it has not, he/she should determine why. In chronological order, the coach should evaluate, first: whether the instructions have been applied correctly by the athlete, and second: whether the quality of execution is lacking. If 'no' in the first instance and/or 'yes' in the second, he/she should check whether his/her objective has been poorly expressed or whether his/her procedure was deficient. Depending on his/her observations and his/her evaluation, the coach should make the appropriate changes to eventually attain the objective set. Table 1 presents a summary of the elements to be taken into account when developing a drill. Also, an example of the structure of a drill, as presented by Mr. Pierre Berjaud (1980), is illustrated in Table 2.

CONCLUSION

The choice and structure of drills is one of the coach's most important tasks. In closing, we draw the attention of coaches to the following points:

o It is important to properly prepare your drills in relation to your actual clientèle.

o Always establish an objective when doing a drill.

o A drill that focusses on qualitative performance should stress technical execution of the skill to be executed, based on certain reference points.

o Avoid having your players inactive during drills - the player must come into contact with the ball as often as possible if he/she is to improve.

o It is important to respect the spatial aspect of the court, the phases of play and the sequences used in a game. The elements specific to volleyball should be observed.

TABLE 1: STRUCTURE OF A DRILL

OBJECTIVE	CONTEXT AND CONDITIONS	SUCCESS CRITERIA	INDICATORS REFERENCE POINTS	EVALUATION

- Clearly define the objective or main element	- Choose the appropriate procedures
	
	- Procedures:
	
	  * Number of players
	
	  * Movement of the players
	
	  * Path of the ball
	
	  * Spatial placement of the player
	
	  * Number of series, repetitions
	
	  * Variants of the drill
		- Success criteria to determine whether the objective has been reached	- What indicators should be used?
			- Reference points related to the task to be accomplished
				- Has the objective been reached?
				
				  * Application of instructions
				
				  * Quality of execution
				
				  * Formulation of the objective
				
				  * Inappropriate procedure

TABLE 2: SAMPLE DRILL (BERJAUD, 1980)

OBJECTIVE	CONTEXT AND CONDITIONS	SUCCESS CRITERIA	INDICATORS REFERENCE POINTS	EVALUATION

- Block: speed of reaction and timing of jump	(diagram: C, A, B positions)
	
	- 3 players:
	
	  * 2 on 1 side with a ball
	  * 1 blocker
	
	"A" attacks a ball he tosses to himself
	
	"C" jumps to block
	
	"B" attacks in turn
	
	- C must block 10 times
	
	<u>Variants</u>
	
	- C has his back to the net - the coach give the signal
	
	- A tosses the ball - C jumps once before blocking
		- The blocker must block the ball 6 out of 10 times	- Blocker's attitude before the block	

SUMMARY

Although drills can be broadly classified as general, specific or competition drills, a volleyball oriented classification would be more precise as such:

- simple drills

- combined drills

- drills of simple action sequences

- complex drills

- drills of complex action sequences

- formation drills

- game drills

Each of these categories of drills plays a specific role in the technical development of a volleyball player.

A coach should prepare drills according to the needs of his/her players/team.

Each drill should be evaluated, so corrective measures can be implemented if the objective has not been reached.

BIBLIOGRAPHY

Berjaud, P.   Automatisation, Consolidation, Stabilisation du contre. STAGE
                   NIVEAU III. Montreal: F.V.B.Q., 1980, pp. 216-218.

Berjaud, P.   La pratique cyclique d'entraînement. Les CAHIERS DE
                   L'ENTRAINEUR. No. 5, Paris: F.V.B.Q., 1979, pp. 17-27.

Cardinal, C.   La formation technique du joueur de volley-ball. CAHIER DE
                   L'ENTRAINEUR I. Montreal: F.V.B.Q., 1983, pp. 141-146.

Cardinal, C.   Course notes, D.H.F.K., Leipzig, G.D.R., 1978.

Morin, G.   Comportement de l'entraîneur à l'entraînement. STAGE NIVEAU
                   III. Montreal: F.V.B.Q., 1978, pp. 113-125.

Pelletier, C.   Préparation d'une séance d'entraînement, STAGE NIVEAU III.
                   Montreal: F.V.B.Q., 1981, pp. 115-126.

THE TRAINING SESSION

By Charles H. Cardinal

THE TRAINING SESSION

The training session is the basic way of developing technique, and developing and maintaining an athlete's state of training of performance factors.

Therefore, the coach should have some knowledge related to conducting efficient training sessions.

Upon completion of this unit, the coach will have a better understanding of the following:

- factors influencing the contents and form of the session

- coaching tasks and general principles involved

- means of outlining the objectives and tasks of the session

- structure of a training session

FACTORS INFLUENCING THE CONTENTS AND FORM OF A TRAINING SESSION

The contents and form of a training session and the training load imposed on an athlete are influenced by the following parameters.

- The development profile of participants involved in the activity: as a coach, do you train beginners, youth, advanced or top level performers? Do you coach growing young people or adults?

- Experience of an athlete: what volume of training have the athletes undertaken to date? What is the quality and the number of competitions participated in? As a substitute or a regular player?

- Actual state of training of athletes: a coach aims to develop or to maintain each component of the state of training of performance factors, that is physical qualities necessary for performance, skill efficiency, tactical capacities and aptitudes, ethical and personal qualities, and tactical intelligence, and above all, to coordinate them to obtain the highest level of performance. Where are your athletes on this continuum?

- The present period, stage, macrocycle, and microcycle: according to your annual training and competition plan, where are you in the schedule? What is the length, frequency, and type of competitions? Have you a peak to be reached in the year, or are competitions spread out over several months and contribute to the final standing?

- Immediate objectives sought: is the objective of the training session, within a microcycle, learning, development, maintenance, or control? Have you several different training tasks within a session?

COACHING TASKS

It could be advantageous at this stage to be aware of coaching tasks during training, to discover the extent of knowledge, skills, and attitudes required by a coach to be efficient in his/her work:

- inform athletes about the objectives and tasks of the training session
- explain and demonstrate the exercises
- teach or consolidate skills and tactics
- ensure exercises are done properly in the main part of the lesson
- observe and detect physical, technical, and tactical problems in athletes
- communicate and intervene to correct the athletes actions, to give and receive feedback
- handle the ball in various situations
- control warm-up, training performance, and cool-down

A quick look at these tasks shows the need for a coach to acquire:

- knowledge about athletics
- knowledge about training
- communication and teaching skills
- knowledge in related fields

GENERAL PRINCIPLES

Let's spend a few minutes going over some general principles which can guide a coach in his/her job.

- Each training session is linked to a training microcycle which has its own logic, objectives, and major emphasis.

- Determine the training load in terms of volume and intensity in a training session, in relation to the microcycle.

- In a training session, the choice of exercises and the training load depend on the task to be fulfilled.

- A coach must plan and orient the training session towards the objective of the microcycle and/or session. General rule: a coach aims to increase an athlete's state of training or to stabilize his/her adaptations.

- A coach must ensure that the activities carried out by an athlete during a session, meet or surpass the requirements of a regulation match. This repertoire includes the sequence and frequency with which skills and tactical movements are done, as well as the particularities of physical effort and nervous stimulation. It is necessary that the body of an athlete be able to go quickly, without negative consequences, from a relative rest period to an effort of optimal intensity and vice-versa, several times during a match (Popescu, 1980).

- While conducting a training session, as far as procedures are concerned, a coach can strive for the following progression:

  - EXPLANATION - DEMONSTRATION of WHAT TO DO and HOW
  - APPLICATION using a choice of appropriate exercises
  - FEEDBACK: does the athlete come closer to imitating the model?

- A coach tries to use the alternating principle:
  - work - rest
  - simple - complex
  - easy - difficult
  - heavy load - light load
  - stimulation and concentration - relaxation
  - muscle groups used

- From a psychological point of view, a coach must ensure the athlete is given a variety of stimuli, while always guaranteeing a high success rate (70% and higher) so that the learning process takes place (Brunelle, 1980).

- If the task is one of acquisition, a coach must ensure that the athlete is actively involved in the work from a motor and cognitive point of view (Brunelle, 1980). Furthermore, an increased volume of repetitions with an adequate recovery period is required.

- Regarding progression, a coach must restrain or slow down an athlete who wants to go too fast. The principle is to gradually and progressively increase the difficulty and complexity of the task.

OBJECTIVES, TASKS, AND METHODS

Each training session is like a small puzzle piece interwoven with another one, and which prepares for the next one, in much the same way a puzzle is done, to form one cohesive piece in a microcycle. A training session can also be described as a scene in a theatrical play, unique, and exclusive by itself but closely and intimately related to the play of which it is a part.

Developing the objective or main theme of a session is influenced by the factors previously mentioned and must take into consideration the general principles set out. This first stage is equivalent to the work a coach wants to accomplish in a session.

Examples: Skill acquisition

or, specific physical preparation and consolidation of skill
or, individual tactics and integration into a system of play with specialization, etc.

The second stage is characterized by determining specific objectives, that is the tasks to be carried out by the athlete. They are realistic and accessible tasks which can be quantified and measured. These tasks must be clearly identified. This stage will determine the specific role of the athlete, a precise activity related task.

Examples: Controlling the spiking action

or, reaction speed and jump timing
or, sending seven out of ten service receptions towards the setter's zone near the net
or, reducing the number of negative comments between players compared to the previous week
or, increasing the number of positive reinforcements among players compared to the previous session
etc.

After developing these two stages, let us briefly review the progression proposed in the chapter CHOICE AND STRUCTURE OF EXERCISES. Once the specific objectives or tasks are identified, a coach defines the context and conditions for realizing each task. This brings a choice of appropriate exercises, characterized by the explanation of the procedure for each exercise. Following are the components of this third stage, for a volleyball exercise: number of players involved in the exercise, position and spatial orientation of players, circulation of the ball, movement of players, number of repetitions and series, and exercise variations.

The fourth stage refers to the establishment of success criteria for determining if an objective was attained or the task adequately realized. These criteria can be quantitative, such as seven successful attacks out of ten. They can be qualitative, emphasizing accuracy such as attacking a specific location/a predetermined target or emphasizing the best motor response, as the choice of the attack skill (spike, tipped ball, playing off the hands of the blocker) appropriate to the situation at hand.

The following stage calls for identifying points of reference or indicators which allow a coach to observe an athlete's movements during the exercise; these are indicators of technique, of proper execution of movement.

The last stage consists of evaluating if a specific objective was reached. If not, a coach must find the reason. Was the objective poorly spelled out? Was the procedure inadequate? Was it because of a lack of explanations? An incomplete demonstration or one that did not conform to the mental image we wanted to create? A task that was too difficult or complex for the athlete's level of realization? A misunderstood task? Etc. After defining the problem, a coach must find the proper corrective answer to help an athlete progress according to the theme of the session.

Look at an example by Pierre Berjaud (1980) which can help clarify the process followed by a coach. The theme of the session is: familiarization with a skill under easy and constant conditions.

Table 1: EXAMPLE OF AN EXERCISE
(Berjaud, 1980)

Specific object-ives or tasks	Context and Conditions for Realization	Success Criteria	Indicators and points of reference	Evalua-tion
Controlling the attack action	1 ball for 2 players One hits the ball, the other catches it 2 series of 10 VARIATIONS - The ball is thrown and hit by the same player - Hit the ball to the floor - The ball is thrown by the other player and then hit a) without jumping b) while jumping	The ball must be controlled by the partner	Position of ball in rela-tion to the body center line Height of the hit	

STRUCTURE OF THE TRAINING SESSION

WELCOME AND INTRODUCTION

A coach must:

-   be present when the athletes arrive. Through informal discussion, he/she must become aware of their attitudes and behaviour

-   try to develop habits such as punctuality and discipline

-   try to show that he/she is well organized and knows what he/she is doing

-   announce objectives and tasks and bring attention to essential points and particular details

-   make sure an athlete clearly understands the objectives and major points of the training session so that he/she can train conscienciously, intensively, and as independently as possible

-   make an athlete understand that the training session is part of a larger plan (microcycle)

-   try to create a climate where an athlete can start training properly through good communication

-   end the meeting on an enjoyable note (example: team cheer)

THE WARM-UP

The goal of the warm up is to prepare an athlete for solving certain athletic tasks through physical exercises.

It is important to note that a warm-up is indispensable because a body, for reasons of efficiency, is regulated to normal performances and that elevated and sudden requirements can cause injuries or reduce the effectiveness of the stimuli.

Two types of warm-ups are used: the general warm-up and the specific warm-up.

The General Warm-Up

- Goal: To prepare all systems in the body for the effort, and to arouse interest and improve the frame of mind towards performing.

- Method: General exercises to:

    - increase mobility to its best
    - relax muscular contractions

    Varied exercises:

    - easy running
    - flexibility exercises
    - stretching exercises

- Specific Load: Low intensity to start with, then progressively and gradually increased.

- Principles: A relaxed warm-up, close to a game, with reduced effort.

- Length: Between 20 and 40 minutes. This depends on:

    - the first main task
    - the temperature of the room
    - the nervous state of players
    - the state of mind

A coach should note that if the first main task consists of speed exercises or a maximal strength effort, the body must be taken gradually to optimal intensity. If the first main task concerns learning technical details or improving the reaction speed, the nervous system should reach its optimal state of stimulation. Furthermore, a warm-up is less complicated when basic endurance is developed with cyclical exercises in the main part of the session.

Specific Warm-Up

- Goal: To prepare an athlete for the particular requirements of an activity:

    - skills
    - reaction capacity
    - concentration

- Principles: Competition movements which are as real as possible

- Method: Working with the ball

MAIN PART

The main part of a training session includes tasks whereby an athlete is able to consolidate or improve state of training.

The contents will be determined by the objective of the session, for example:

- to develop or maintain general physical qualitites
- to develop or maintain specific physical qualities
- to acquire, improve, or stabilize skills
- to acquire, improve, or stabilize tactics
- to form ethical and personal qualities
- to develop tactical intelligence

If a training session includes several of these tasks, the main part must have the following sequential order:

- 1st stage: tasks for skill development
- 2nd stage: development of speed
- 3rd stage: development of endurance

First Stage: Solving Tasks for Skill Development with Medium Effort

Learning new elements of skills or familiarization with a skill requires a lot of concentration on the part of an athlete. Maintaining this kind of concentration is only possible when the nervous system is not tired. Furthermore, "the development and differentiation of newly conditioned motor reflexes work positively only when the nervous system is in a state of optimal excitation" (Cardinal, 1978). Acquisition of a skill or fault correction requires a low to medium effort, while in consolidation and stabilization, the skill should be combined with specific physical preparation or performed under conditions close to that of competition.

A coach should be aware of certain principles which guide a player's learning:

- active participation of the player in the activity
- a large number of contacts with the ball
- a success rate of 70% or more (Brunelle, 1980)

Because of the levels of concentration and nervous stimulation required of a player, it is necessary that the participant be fresh and in good condition, to facilitate a high rate of success in the exercise. Thus, the importance of putting the development of technique in the first stage of the main part of the training session.

Second Stage: Development of Speed

The reaction time and speed of movement are two important physical qualities for realizing a performance in volleyball. Acquiring a repertoire of dynamic and automatic motorskills is an important preliminary condition to the development and improvement of reaction speed.   This development occurs by gradually and progressively increasing the difficulty and complexity of the task.

Examples:

- Solving certain simple standard situations at a reduced, medium, and high speed

- Solving conventional tasks while increasing the number of possible responses (example: two types of defence)

- Solving unexpected tasks

- Solving situations where the degree of difficulty is above the requirements for competition (example: balls hit against an uneven wall so they will rebound in an unpredictable way)

To reach our objective, exercises emphasizing speed are effectively stimulating only if the body is not tired and is able to function optimally. Emphasizing speed at the end of a fatiguing task or session, does not contribute to development of pure speed, but helps to improve the qualities of endurance speed and willpower.

A player's speed of execution calls for explosive strength which, in turn rests on the maximal muscular strength of a player. Therefore, an increase in muscular strength must also be combined with increased speed of execution. A coach should create conditions which allow for particularly quick muscular contraction. When exercises are being carried out, it is necessary to increase the rhythm, while always requiring that execution be technically correct and efficient. "It is important to stress that a speed which is higher than those attained until now, depends on the level of willpower of a player" (Cardinal, 1978).

Third Stage: Development of Endurance

Because of the length of our competitions (marathon tournaments or 3 out of 5 matches), the continual change in the intensity of movements, the numerous interruptions between play sequences or matches, volleyball places high demand on aerobic capacity as well as anaerobic capacity. The load then becomes the interval type, and endurance training must take into account these specific conditions. We must develop endurance in volleyball through specific athletic methods and in close relationship with resolving the technical-tactical tasks. This can also be done through the duration principle and the interval principle. "In specific endurance training for competition, it is necessary above all to use medium and short interval methods. The total length of a load can be a bit above the length of competition, medium intensity being specific to competition or a little bit higher (Cardinal, 1978).

Examples:

- Short interval: Length of individual load varies from 15 seconds to 2 minutes

- Medium interval: Length of individual load varies from 2 to 8 minutes

- Circuit training:

    - Load: 3 to 5% of body weight
    - Repetition of series: 20 - 40% of repetitions of movements necessary for competition
    - Speed of movement - continuous to fast
    - Rest: optimal
    - Series: 4 to 6

CALM-DOWN

For the calm-down period, use the following principles:

- training must not end immediately after a heavy workout

- an increase or decrease in load must be done gradually, never abruptly

- carefully bring the body to its normal functioning state, by progressively decreasing intensity and/or by reducing the concentration required. This helps to spare the body, accelerates the recovery process and helps an athlete move on to other tasks.

- the session is finished with a pleasant conversation, which includes a brief analysis of the session

- never leave the training site with any aggressive feelings

ANALYSIS OF TRAINING

In order that a training session fill its pedagogical purposes and to fully guarantee orientation of the training process, it is necessary to do a post-analysis, even if it is short. Training loses its efficiency if we do not draw any conclusions. A coach constantly needs information on the relationships between the work provided during training and on the current physical and psychological condition and level of performance of the athlete. Increasing the state of training depends on a number of factors which are often only recognized during training. Analysis after a session is to verify the efficiency of training and to discover any sources of trouble. This analysis becomes indispensable to the progress and efficiency of training and is a preliminary condition for planning future training.

SUMMARY

- The training session's load and contents are influenced by factors related to the type of athletes involved and to the tasks to be accomplished.

- The coach has numerous tasks in conducting a session. He/she will perform better if he/she plans the session carefully.

- For each exercise, the coach should establish objectives, success criteria and points of reference for evaluation of performance.

- Each session should be composed of a warm-up, main part and cool-down.

- If the session includes several tasks, the main part must have the following sequential order:

  - 1st Stage: Tasks for Skill Development
  - 2nd Stage: Development of Speed
  - 3rd Stage: Development of Endurance

- An analysis of the training session, however brief, will bring useful conclusions for the planning of future sessions.

BIBLIOGRAPHY

COACHING ASSOC.   Level I Coaching Theory, National Coaching
OF CANADA   Certification Program, Ottawa.

BERJAUD, P.   Automatisation, consolidation et stabilisation du contre, Stage niveau III. Montreal: F.V.B.Q., 1980, pp. 212-218.

BERJAUD, P.   La préparation physique, Stage niveau III. Montreal: F.V.B.Q., 1980, pp. 132-145.

BRUNELLE, J.   Projet de recherche, Laval University, Quebec: Summer 1980.

CARDINAL, C.H.   La séance d'entraînement, Niveau I. Montreal: F.V.B.Q., 1980.

CARDINAL, C.H.   Notes de cours, D.H.F.K., Leipzig: R.D.A. 1978.

PELLETIER, C.   Préparation d'une séance d'entraînement, Stage niveau III. Montreal: F.V.B.Q., 1981, pp. 115-126.

POPESCU, A.   Les caractéristiques de la leçon, Notes de cours, D.E.P., Université de Montréal, 1980.

FOOTWORK AND
POSITIONING

By: Claude Pelletier
Keith Wasylik

FOOTWORK AND

POSITIONING

It has often been stated that "a structure is only as good as its foundation". Volleyball skills follow the same principle, and are developed on a sound basis of good footwork.

Upon completion of this section, coaches will have a better understanding of:

- The basic, or ready position

- Court movement characteristics

- Court movement principles

- Patterns and types of movement

NOTE: While respecting the same basic principles, there are distinct trends of application. We have included in this article such a different application under the caption "Variation".

BASIC POSITION

The basic or fundamental position is characterized not only by the correct positioning of the body segments, but primarily by an attitude of energy and preparedness to act. This position is the same for most technical moves; it consists of assuming a comfortable, dynamic position that will enable the player to move in any direction and be in a position to play the ball correctly: in other words, balanced over the feet. The basic position should ensure the functional arrangement of the body segments to enable the player to take off quickly in a given direction.

PRINCIPLES

The Feet

Figure 1

- The feet are parallel or oriented slightly inwards.

- The distance between the feet (side-to-side or front-to-back) should allow for the weight of the body to be evenly distributed over the feet. Thus, the support base will vary depending on the athlete's sex, size and length of body segments. The athlete must be as comfortable as possible.

- The body weight is distributed over the forward, inside part of the feet. The knees are also bent slightly inward.

- In the basic position, the pelvis and feet should be aligned. The pelvis is thus directly over the feet. As a result, the knees will be positioned ahead of the feet.

The Trunk

- The trunk and the pelvis are interdependent.
- The trunk is upright or inclined slightly forward.
- The height of the centre of gravity should depend on the player's position on the court. Thus, the basic position varies depending on whether the athlete is playing the back of the court, along an angle, or close to the net.

The Arms

- The arms and shoulders should be relaxed.
- The elbows are held close to the body.
- The hands may be clasped or separate. Some athletes tend to play with the hands clasped while others tend to leave them apart. A number of players, on receiving serve, prepare their hands and arms before the serve is executed. It is noted, however, that players playing defence prefer not to have one hand held in the other as this restricts their freedom of positioning and movement on the court.

COURT MOVEMENTS

CHARACTERISTICS

- "Proper positioning allows for proper movement" (Cassignol).
- The ball is first played with the feet. To play the ball correctly, the athletes must first position themselves under the ball, which implies movement on the court.
- All such movements must be designed so that the player plays the ball on balance over the feet and not thrown out of position.
- Movements are related to the spatiotemporal context (i.e. to the direction, speed, path and dropping point of the ball and also to the place and nature of the ball's return within an area of play).
- In any movement, there is an orientation phase and a positioning phase of the two last steps.

PRINCIPLES

Based on these points, we can say that there are five main principles that govern the use of court movements:

Shifting of Weight

The main principle governing the use of court movements in volleyball is that of the shifting of weight.

When players want to move in a particular direction, they must, before they even move a foot or leg, shift the weight of their body onto the leg on the side to which they will move.

Variation: *When players wants to move in a particular direction, they must first slightly lift the foot or the leg on the side to which they will move.*

4-4

Movement of the Lead Foot

The second principle is the outcome of the shifting of weight. This first step can be characterized as being for orientation.

The first foot that moves is the foot away from the direction of the movement, or further from the dropping point of the ball. For example, in moving to the right, the athlete first shifts weight and then takes the first step with the left foot.

Variation: *The first foot that moves is the foot closest to the direction of the movement. For example, in moving to the right, the athlete first lifts the right foot slightly and then takes the first step with the right foot.*

Movement at a 45° Angle

All movements are structured around a 45° angle from the basic position.

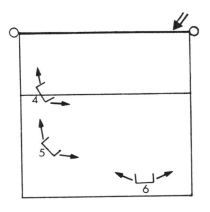

Figure 2

- The positioning of the player on the court should promote this 45° movement to enable the players to intercept the ball more easily.

- Also, the playing of the ball is structured around a 45° movement, because it is easier to cover the various angles of attack and attack opportunities (in relationship to the block).

Final Positioning of the Feet

The movement is completed by the final orientation of the feet to promote a positioning of the pelvis towards the target and the inner court.

The second-last step to promote blocking and body movement for a ball return, should include an inclining of the body in the direction of the ball return, rather than in the direction of the court movement. The trailing foot (outer foot) will make it easier to position the pelvis in the direction of the return, being brought in front of the other. The distribution of body weight over the feet will be about 60% over the front leg and 40% over the back leg; this distribution will allow for better orientation of the body on contact and will make last minute adjustments easier if necessary.

Variation: *The second-last step to promote blocking and body movement for a ball return, includes an inclining of the body in direction of the return. The lead foot is already in front so the hips should be quite easily squared to the target. The distribution of body weight may be 60-40% but a slight split-hop just prior to the opponent contacting the ball will bring the centre of gravity in line, and the body in balance.*

Timing of Movement and Final Positioning of the Feet

To illustrate this, let us take the example of a defence player who must recover a ball. Movement is initiated on first contact of the ball by the opposing team. At that moment, the stationary player shifts his/her body weight to the leg on the side to which he/she intends to move. While the offence player sets the ball, the defence player moves to the appropriate position, depending on the possible angles of attack for the territory he/she is covering. The defence player must synchronize his/her last two steps so that the feet are positioned as, or immediately after, the attacker hits the ball. The placement of the feet will enable the player to have a fairly broad lift base (side-to-side or forward-to-back), with the correct distribution of body weight (60%-40%). As contact with the ball must be made directly over the feet, the positioning of the feet should also promote this distribution ratio.

Variation: *Just before, or as the attacker hits the ball, the feet should split under and help lower the centre of gravity. This will enable the player to have a stable support base.*

PATTERNS AND TYPES OF MOVEMENT

The pattern and type of movement used will be determined by the speed and trajectory of the ball. The player will have to cover a certain distance in order to be able to play the ball directly over the feet. The movement will be short or long depending on the distance between the player and the ball. It should also be pointed out that the last steps are steps to gain position, not steps to cover distance, so that when players contact the ball, they must be in a steady, balanced position.

Two-Step Movement

A common movement pattern in volleyball is the two-step movement. Once the weight has been transferred, the feet are positioned right-left or left-right depending on the player's position on the court and the movement to the ball. In this movement structure, the lead leg must serve both for orientation and positioning.

The rhythm of the positioning of the feet will be determined primarily by the speed and path of the ball. A ball travelling along a more direct path or at greater speed will force the player to move more quickly.

In relation to this pattern, there are three conventional types of movement - forward, backward and lateral.

Forward Movement

In forward movement, the player moves the lead foot according to his/her position on the court and the point to which he/she is to return the ball.

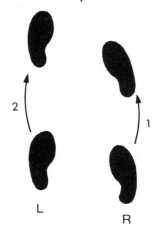

Figure 3:
Two-step forward movement
on the left of the court.

- Forward movement to the left of the court (Figure 3).

- The players transfer their weight to the left leg and the weight of the body will be slightly forward, ready to move forwards.

- They first move their right foot (1) forward and complete their movement by then placing their left foot (2) ahead of the right. The forward foot points in the direction of the pass.

Forward movement to the right of the court (Figure 4). The player transfers their weight to the right leg and their body weight is shifted forward, ready to move forwards.

They first move their left foot (1) forward. They then complete their movement by placing their right foot (2) ahead of the left and pointing in the direction of the pass.

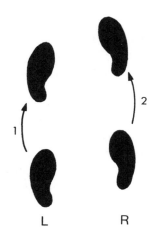

Figure 4:
Two-step forward movement
to the right of the court.

Backward Movement

The principles of backward movement are the same. First, the weight is shifted to the right leg. The left foot (1) is moved first. The right foot (2) is then moved back and positioned so that the body is oriented in the direction of the pass.

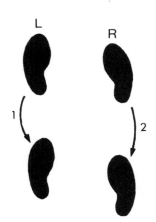

Figure 5

Lateral Movement

For lateral movement in volleyball, the player uses the crossover. The crossover is the most important type of movement in volleyball, and the one that should be favoured. Let us look at two examples of crossover movements from a defensive position in position 5.

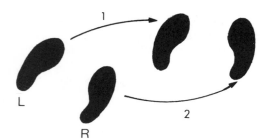

To move to the right (Figure 6), the players shift their body weight to the right leg. The left foot moves first and crosses over in front of the right foot (1). Once the body weight has been transferred to the left leg, the right foot passes behind the left foot and comes to rest so as to orient the body in the direction of the pass.

To move to the left, the players shift their body weight to the left leg. The right foot moves first and crosses over in front of the left foot (1). Once the body weight has been transferred to the right leg, the left foot passes behind the right foot and comes to rest so as to orient the body in the direction of the pass.

In some situations where the distance to be covered is relatively short, the player will not necessarily need to execute a full crossover (Figure 7). So the left foot comes to rest in line with the right (1). The right foot then moves to the right and comes to rest so as to orient the pelvis in the desired direction (2).

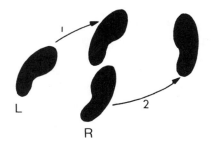

Figure7

Three-Step Movement (1-2-3)

There is another movement pattern in volleyball known as the three-step movement. This pattern is also present in attack and block moves, and is used in other play activity such as service reception, defensive play, and particularly for movements over a greater distance. It can, however, very well be learned as the basic pattern of all movements. Most importantly, it should be noted that the first step in this movement structure is for orientation, whereas the other two are for positioning.

The structure of the three-step movement is characterized by a hop on the second step, which may be shorter or longer depending on the trajectory of the ball. The rhythm of the foot movement in the three-step movement is characterized by rapid positioning of the last two steps. Even though these two steps are not taken simultaneously (2-3), floor contact is almost simultaneous.

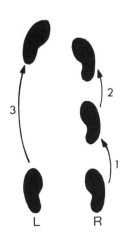

Figure 8

Figure 8 shows forward three-step movement. This is a case of serve reception in position 5.

The players must first shift their weight to the front portion of the left leg.

This enables them to then step the right foot forward (1).

They then hop on the same foot, that is, on the right foot (2) and, finally, the left foot is brought slightly forward and set down so as to orient the body in the direction of the pass (3).

The player in position 6 first shifts his/her body weight to the right foot. The left foot moves first, crossing over in front of the right foot (1). Once the body weight has been transferred to the left leg, the player hops on the left foot (2). This hop will be long or short depending on the dropping point of the ball. During this hop, the right foot crosses over behind the left leg and then moves quickly so as to orient the body in the direction of the pass (3).

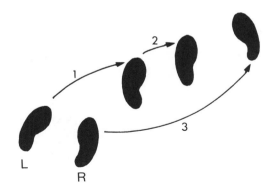

Figure 9:
Lateral three-step
movement to the right

Movement of Four or More Steps

To recover a ball that is very far away, the player uses a more advanced three-step pattern. It is impossible to say how many steps are needed in these movements. It can, however, be said that this pattern is also based on the basic principles governing the use of movements.

Two examples of this pattern are lateral movement to the right (Figure 10) and movement to the back court (Figure 11).

For a lateral movement to the right (Figure 10) over a very great distance, the players must first shift their body weight to the right leg. They then take off with their left leg as the body simultaneously pivots. The last two steps are for positioning and stability. Thus, the last step is placed ahead and outside so as to orient the body in the direction of the ball return.

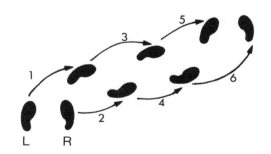

Figure 10:
Movement to the right,
consisting of a number of steps

In the case of movement to the back court, and in the following example (Figure 11), to the left back court, the players must first shift their body weight to the right leg. The left foot (1) is moved first to promote the turning of the body. Then, the body's position is changed by positioning the right foot (2) so as to orient the body in the direction of the run.

The last two steps (3-4) are positioned successively so as to orient the body towards the ball return. In this situation, the player does not have time to position themself to play the ball facing the net. They should, then, contact the ball with their back to the net, in an attempt to place the ball so that a teammate can continue the play.

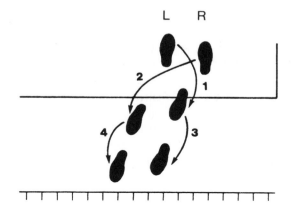

Figure11:
Movement to the back court,
consisting of a number of steps

The examples in Figures 10 and 11 illustrating movements consisting of more than three steps, rarely occur in a game situation. It is, therefore, not necessary to spend hours learning these techniques. It is preferable for the coach to devote hours of training to the acquisition, stabilization and consolidation of the techniques of two- and three-step movements, which are used in most situations encountered in volleyball.

COMMON FAULTS, ERRORS AND CORRECTIONS

FAULT	ERRORS	CORRECTIONS
Basic Position		
Centre of Gravity too high	a) Feet are too close together b) Pelvis too far forward	1,2,3 1,2,3
Body Weight on heels	a) Feet pointing out b) Pelvis too far back c) Knees straight d) Hands too low	1,2,3 1,2,3 1,2,3 1,2,3
Stiff upper body	a) Shoulders contracted too much b) Too much forward/backward body lean	1,2,3 1,2,3
Movements		
Lead with wrong foot	a) Incorrect weight shift	1,2,3
Poor balance	a) Poor foot orientation b) Poor foot position c) Body weight outside the base of support d) Steps are too slow	1,2,3,4,5 1,2,3,4,5 1,2,3,4,5 1,2,3,4

CORRECTIONS

1) Coach physically manipulates body parts to correct posture
2) Use mirror
3) Video
4) Use slow rolling balls to force athletes to step with better orientation and point into ball
5) Have athlete carry ball in hands to stress a forward lean into the pass

DRILLS

These drills are designed to teach the player correct movement.

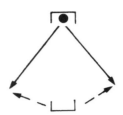

Figure 12

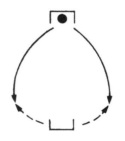

Figure 13

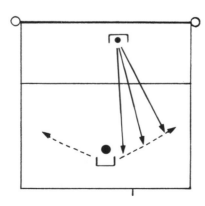

Figure 14

1. The ball is rolled along the floor by a teammate. The player rolls it back to him/her along the floor. Begin with slow movements over short distances. When the athlete has mastered the move, the coach increases the speed slightly and imposes a normal distance of travel.

2. Now concentrate on the use of the correct starting foot.

3. Now concentrate on movement at a 45° angle.

4. Now concentrate on orientation of the last two steps

5. Now vary the types of movement.

6. Working in pairs, the player lobs the ball to the right or left, about 1 metre from the player.

7. Now toss the ball about 2 metres from the player.

8. Now toss the ball about 3 metres from the player.

9. From behind a boundary, a player moves to catch a ball tossed by a teammate. He/she returns the ball to the thrower and goes back to his/her position behind the boundary.

10. Now vary the distances (short and long).

11. Now the thrower tosses the ball so as to drill the player's speed of movement:

   - by decreasing the time between throws
   - by altering the path of the ball (semi-direct or direct ball)
   - by increasing the ball speed

These drills are designed to teach the player to move to pass the ball correctly.

1. Player begins in position #6, the coach tosses the ball to the left, then the right. The player must return the ball using a forearm pass.

2. Coach now lob spikes the ball.

3. Coach now spikes the ball.

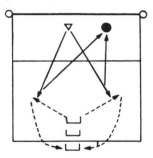

Figure 15

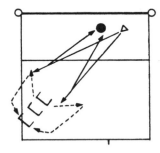

Figure 16

4. Coach tosses the ball to position #5, to the left and right of the player.

    Player returns ball using a forearm pass.

5. Coach now lob spikes the ball.

6. Coach now spikes the ball

7. Coach tosses the ball to position #1, to the left and right of the player.

    Player returns ball using a forearm pass.

8. Coach now lob spikes the ball.

9. Coach now spikes the ball.

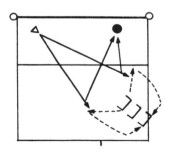

Figure 17

10. Coach tosses two balls in succession.

    Player must move and return both balls using forearm passes, starting in position #6.

11. Coach spikes first ball, tosses second ball.

12. Player starts in position #5.

13. Player starts in position #1.

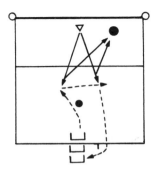

Figure 18

SUMMARY

- The basic position is a comfortable, dynamic position that will enable the player to move in any direction and be in a position to play the ball correctly.

- Court movement characteristics include:

  - Movement with the feet
  - Playing the ball while squarely over the feet
  - Movement which is related to the path of the ball
  - Movement involving an orientation and a positioning phase

- The five principles of court movement are:

  - Shifting of weight
  - Movement of the lead foot
  - Movement at a 45° angle
  - Final positioning of the feet
  - Timing of movement

- Three types of movement are:

  - Two-step movement
  - Three-step movement
  - Four or more steps

THE FOREARM PASS

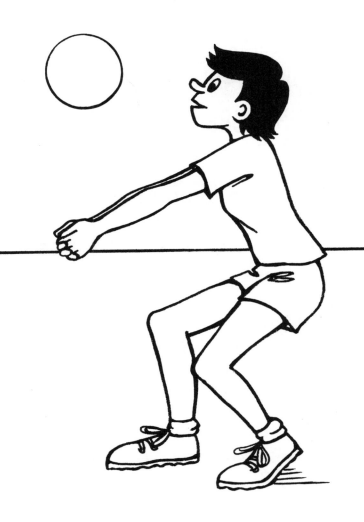

By Keith Wasylik

THE FOREARM PASS

The ability to pass a ball with the forearms is perhaps the most crucial skill in the game of volleyball. Often it is the forearm pass, especially on serve reception, which determines the level of play in a volleyball match. This section deals with the fundamental forearm pass. A clear understanding of this skill is necessary before moving on to the more complex skills required in playing defence.

Upon completion of this section, coaches will have a better understanding of the following:

- the body mechanics of the forearm pass

- the movement skills necessary to pass the ball efficiently

The fundamental forearm pass described in this section may be used in game situations primarily to:

- receive and pass the serve

Other uses include to:

- receive the opponents attack

- pass an opponents "free" ball

- pass a "difficult" ball (e.g. after a block)

MECHANICS OF THE FOREARM PASS

GETTING READY

The body should be in a relatively erect position with a slight bend forward at the hips. The knees should be flexed so that the body can move efficiently to the ball.

The back is relatively straight and the head held in a natural position. In order to make tracking the ball easier, the head should remain as steady as possible and not raise up or drop dramatically. Try to move the eyes to track the path of the ball.

From the initial ready position, facing the source of the path of the ball, the player should move quickly to a skip-stop to intercept the trajectory of the ball and end up facing the intended target line. (Figure 1)

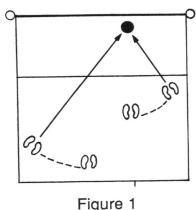

Figure 1

Just prior to contact with the ball, the feet should be wider than shoulder width apart, in a staggered stance, the proper foot should be forward and the feet pointing at the target.

The body should be aligned so that contact with the ball takes place in the <u>midline of the body</u> which is in line with the target.

THE HANDS

The hands should be joined on contact with the ball. They can be brought together by consciously touching either the base of the little fingers, the heel of the hands or the base of the thumbs together.

The fingers can also be joined in numerous ways.

Figure 2

Figure 3

Figure 4

Figure 5

The key to consistent surface in the forearms is the alignment of the thumbs: pressed together, straight and parallel throughout their length (Figure 5).

THE ARMS

It is important that the arms remain away from the body throughout the passing action to allow for the proper contact angle of the arms relative to the ground. For serve reception, the elbows should be close to the trunk and flexed slightly. The starting position could look like either Figure 6 or Figure 7.

Starting Positions

Figure 6

* Elbows flexed; shoulders extended slightly; player "sights ball over thumbs"; body ready to move

* Elbows flexed; shoulders relaxed; body ready to move.

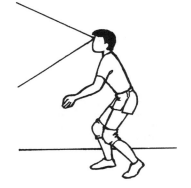

Figure 7

The arms can be straight on contact or still slightly bent to allow for some "give" with the force of the ball contact. Players should position themselves so that the ball contacts both arms equally between the wrists and elbows.

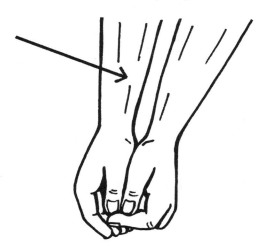

Figure 8
Contact Point

Do not swing the arms forcefully at the ball, but keep the shoulders "slightly tense" in order to provide a good rebounding surface for the ball.

BODY ACTION

Two player mechanics affect the outcome of a forearm pass.

The rebound angle of the arms

The angle of the arms relative to the floor and the path of the incoming ball are two important factors which determine the rebound angle and resultant trajectory of the passed ball.

A small relative angle of the arm to the floor will usually result in a higher trajectory pass. A larger angle will usually result in a "flatter" pass.

The body position and movement through contact

As the ball is being contacted, both knees move forward to bring the hips and upper body (i.e. center of gravity) forward into the ball (Figure 9). It is extremely important that not just the hips "push through the ball", but the entire body moves slightly forward as a flexible unit into the contact.

Figure 9

For a slow moving serve or "free" ball, the passer may have to add some force by stroking (swinging) the arms <u>a little</u> in the direction of the pass.

For a faster moving ball the passer may have to absorb some force by moving the body unit or arms backward on contact.

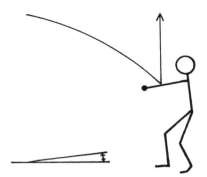

Figure 10
Small angle = high trajectory

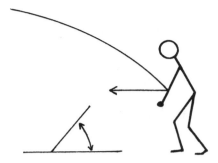

Figure 11
Larger angle = flatter pass

Therefore, in the front half of the court players may wish to play the ball from a lower stance (Figure 12) in order to keep the ball on their side of the net. When a player is close to the net, lowering their center of gravity under the contact of the ball can ensure a good passing/rebounding angle of their arms.

Figure 12

TEACHING PROGRESSSION

The following drills are designed to develop eye/forearm coordination.

<u>Drill 1</u>:   Players each have a balloon and use forearms (R,L, alternate), to keep balloon in the air.

Each player has a ball.

<u>Drill 2</u>:   Player bounces ball off floor, then contact with R forearm, bounce, L forearm, repeat.

<u>Drill 3</u>:   As above, bounces against wall and floor.

<u>Drill 4</u>:   Player bounces ball into air then catch: 2,3,4 consecutive, etc.

    a) R forearm   b) L forearm   c) alternate

The following drills are designed to facilitate the individual player's control of the basic forearm pass.

<u>Drill 5</u>:   Players (without a ball) in scattered formation practice proper skip-stop, foot placement and body action.

Partners, with one ball

<u>Drill 6</u>:

- Player at net tosses easy two-hand-underhand toss to partner who is kneeling on both knees approximately 1-2m away
- Partner should have knees wider than hips to allow body to move forward easier than hips

a) Partner forearm passes ball to land half-way between players
b) Partner passes ball back to tosser

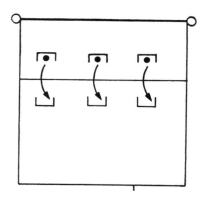

Figure 13

Drill 7:

- Both standing

- Player tosses underhand toss from net and partner moves forward to forearm pass the ball

a) Halfway back to tosser

b) Back to tosser

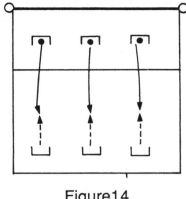

Figure 14

Group of three, one ball

Drill 8:

- 2 players at net, one player approximately 3-4m away

- 1 tosses ball, player 2 starts facing 1

- 2 then moves to intercept ball and turns to face 3, 2 passes to 3

- 2 moves over to start in front of 3, repeat, with cross-court pass to 1

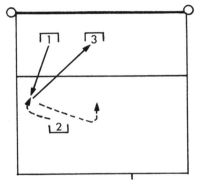

Figure 15

COMMON FAULTS, ERRORS AND CORRECTIONS

Faults	Errors	Corrections
1. Trajectory too vertical Figure 16	* angle of the arms is too shallow relative to the ground: i) player swings arms ii) player extends legs up iii) player leans back on contact iv) foot placement might be too narrow and elongated forward/back	1,2,3
2. Trajectory too flat Figure 17	* angle of the arms is too steep relative to the ground: i) player drops hands between knees prior to contact ii) player extends legs straight up iii) player leans too far forward on contact	1,2,3,4
3. Inconsistent passes -off to one side, ball hits chest, shoulders, etc.	a) poor eye-forearm coordination b) hands not together and/or thumbs not parallel, results in uneven contact surface	1*,2,5,6 *especially beginning contact drills

	c) poor footwork = poor base/body position = difficult to get fore-arms on ball	

CORRECTIONS

1. Re-do part of progression
   - body action without ball

2. Use video and mirrors
   - show error in form
   - show correct form
   - retape player in correct form

3. Place target 1/2 way between tosser and passer and strive for pass <u>only</u> 2-3m high into target, i.e. hulahoop attached to high jump standards or bucket

4. Partners forearm pass ball over a net between them
   = higher trajectory

5. Use gloves that have "velcro" pads at base of thumbs, i.e. conscious effort to get hands/thumbs together

6. Movement/speed drills to get to ball faster and get balance (use slower tossed balls)

DRILLS

The following drills are designed to assist in developing a player's movement to the ball and to pass accurately to a target:

Partners, one ball

<u>Drill 1</u>:

- Players at net toss ball to about mid-court

- Partners start 1m inside baseline, on signal (verbal, ball toss, etc.) sprint forward 3-4 steps, skip-stop, pass ball, return to baseline

- Tosser should evaluate pass, coach evaluate technique/movement

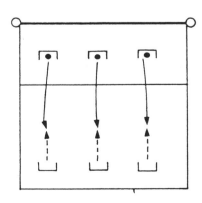

Figure 18

Drill 2:

- Players at net toss ball to mid-court

- Partners start approximately 1m from tosser, on signal move backwards to mid-court, skip-stop, pass ball

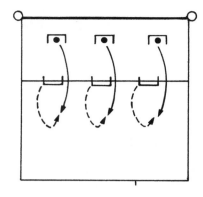

Figure 19

Drill 3:

- Players at net turn feet in any direction, toss ball in that direction

- Partners start at mid-court, on signal (feet) move to one side or other, skip-stop, pass ball.

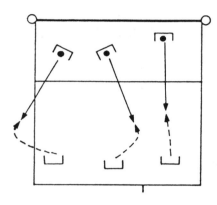

Figure 20

Drill 4: Combine above drills; move forward, pass; cover; move backward, pass; move left, pass; move right, pass; return to start.

Drill 5:

- Group of three, one ball
- 1 at mid-court easy serve or throw ball over net
- 2 approximately mid-court to receive serve and pass ball to 3. 2 should start facing 1, then move to ball and end up facing target (3)
- 3 catch ball (or self volley 1m) and return ball to 1
- Rotate after 10 passes (or time)

* As players skills improve gradually move server back to serving zone.

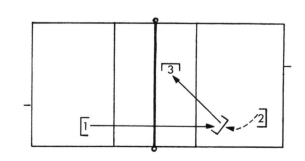

Figure 21

Drill 6:

- Group of four, two balls

a) Self toss and volley across net to backcourt player. Forearm pass to partner at net. Repeat.

b) Same drill, but partner at net sets ball approximately 2-5m high and B comes forward to cover/catch
   - Change places, repeat

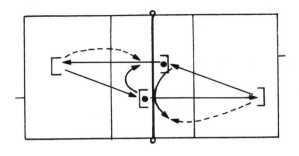

Figure 22

Drill 7:

- One ball

- Same drill as above, but continuous

- Self toss and volley across net, forearm pass, set, approach and volley across net to backcourt player

- Continue (players exchange positions continuously)

Drill 8:

- Group of five, one ball
- Three players at target position by net
- Players at net volley to alternate sides of court,
- Players in backcourt forearm pass ball to target
- Pass, cover, and follow ball to new position
- Players at net become new backcourt passers
- Continue

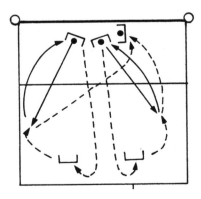

Figure 23

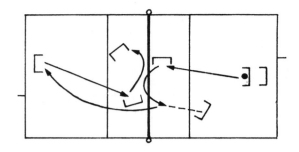

Figure 24

Drill 9:

- Group of seven, one ball
- Start two players at the ball
- Players in backcourt use forearm pass, players at the net volley
- Each player <u>follows the ball</u> to a new position
- Continue

SUMMARY

- Face the source of the ball, move quickly to get ready; <u>then</u> feet, hips and shoulders face the target.

- Be on balance with the feet wider than shoulder width and the trunk in a relatively erect position with a slight flexion in the hips.

- Keep your head natural and the eyes tracking the ball.

- Thumbs/hands start a) as "sights" <u>or</u> b) in front of body and then come together and remain parallel.

- Move the body as a unit (center of gravity) to contact the ball.

- Contact the ball on the forearms between the wrists and elbows.

- Add <u>or</u> absorb force depending on the speed of the ball and the distance from the target.

- Maintain the correct angle in the forearms relative to the ground to ensure accurate trajectory passes.

THE OVERHAND PASS

By: Brad Kilb
Keith Wasylik

THE OVERHAND PASS

Although volleying the ball overhead with the fingers is utilized most commonly by the setter, it is important that every player be able to execute this skill. Not every time will the team pass the ball perfectly to the setter, thus other players might be required to set the ball. When mastered, the volley is a safe and extremely accurate passing skill.

Upon completion of this section, the coach will have a better understanding of the following:

- The body mechanics of the volley

- Movement skills necessary to volley efficiently

The basic skill of volleying may be used in various game situations to:

- Pass "easy" balls

- Set up teammates for an attack

GETTING READY

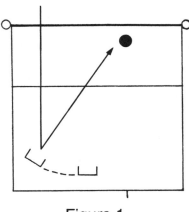

Figure 1

From the ready position the player should <u>move quickly to play the ball</u>, and aim to <u>contact the ball in a direct line between themselves and their target</u>. (Figure 1)

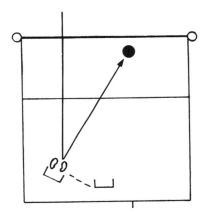

Figure 2:
FOOT PLACEMENT, PRIOR TO CONTACT

The player sets up to play the ball by moving quickly to intercept the ball and using a skip-stop to a <u>staggered stance, with their front foot pointing towards the target</u>. The feet should be comfortable, about shoulder width apart, so the player can maintain good balance.

BODY POSITION

The knees and hips are slightly bent, with the back relatively straight. The <u>head is up</u> with the eyes tracking the ball. The <u>shoulders should be square to the target</u>.

THE ARMS AND HANDS

The hands come up above the eyes so that the arms are bent comfortably with the upper arms parallel to the floor, and about 45° to the shoulder girth.

The hands are held in a △ or ◇ shape, about 8-10cm from the eyes (further if the player has very long limbs). The fingers are spread comfortably and pointing up and back with the thumbs pointing back over the <u>opposite ear</u>. The distance between the thumbs and the distance between the forefingers should be the same or slightly wider between the forefingers. The wrists are cocked back slightly so the player can actually sight the ball through the △ or ◇ formed by the thumbs and forefingers (Figure 3).

Figure 3:
TRACKING BALL THROUGH THE "WINDOW"

BODY ACTION

Prior to contact, the entire body comes into play with a conscious extension of the legs (knees). Hips and arms (elbows) then follow in the direction of the intended trajectory of the pass.

In order to volley a ball backwards the athlete should move the pelvis forward, <u>slightly past</u> the point of contact with the ball, just as the knees begin extension (Figure 4). Remember height is more important than distance.

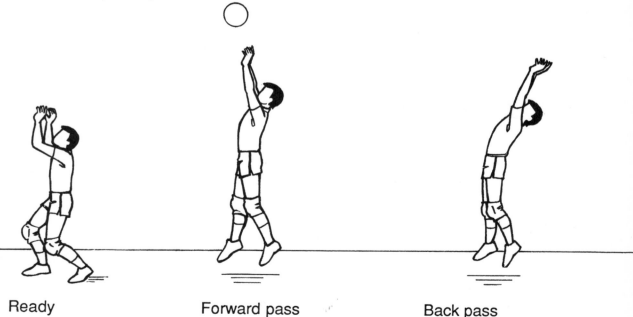

Ready   Forward pass   Back pass

Figure 4

Following this powerful <u>total body "extension" upwards</u> through the ball, the athlete should land on both feet and continue to move in the direction of the pass.

For short distance volleys, the athlete would not have to extend so forcefully and, therefore, the feet would probably remain in contact with the ground.

For teams that require a lower trajectory pass on free ball conversions, the athlete would assume a more elongated forward-back stride position prior to contact and the athlete would use more of a weight transfer movement from his/her back foot to front foot instead of a simultaneous upward extension of both legs.

CONTACT WITH THE BALL

As the body begins its action upward through the ball, the hands begin moving away from the eyes and the fingers and thumbs contact the ball with the fleshy "fingerpads". The fingers should be kept fairly firm. However, as the body extends, the weight of the ball tends to push the thumbs and forefingers back.

Contact should be made on the back part of the ball, with the hands a comfortable and controlable distance apart (depending on the size of the hands). (Figure 5)

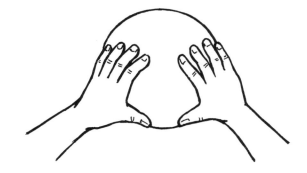

Figure 5: CONTACT WITH THE BALL

TEACHING PROGRESSION

These drills are designed to facilitate the individual's control of the volley as a pass.

Each player has a ball.

1. Kneeling on the floor with a ball in front, place hands on top of the ball in the correct position. Pick up the ball with the correct "grip", <u>look up</u> and place the ball in the correct position 10cm above the eyes.

2. Standing, two hand underhand self-toss and catch in correct volleyball position.

   -coach can check feet, body, hands
   -obviously athlete will have to move to ball if tossing skills are not accurate

3. Toss, bend knees, catch.

4. Toss, bend, start push, catch (use legs only and do not release ball).

5. Toss, bend, start push/catch (legs and arms; release ball).

6. Each player bends over at the waist with a ball;
   With the correct hand position on the top of the ball, the players bounce the ball onto the floor using their arms and wrists.

7. Toss, bend, push/catch (minimize time between the catch and release of the ball).

8. Toss, bend, volley.

9. Toss, bend, volley into a target (i.e. horizontal hoop 2-4m above floor).

10. Players stand about 1m from the wall with a ball. The players volley the ball against the wall, contacting the ball in the correct position each time. Volley 1 and catch; 2,3,4, etc.

11. Players volley to themselves and follow commands of coach:

    - "3 meters high"
    - "one meter"
    - "move in a zig-zag around court"
    - "volley, turn 180˚, volley"
    - "volley, bounce, lie down, volley"
    - "volley, sit, volley, lie down, volley, sit, volley, stand, volley"

COMMON FAULTS, ERRORS AND CORRECTIONS

FAULTS	ERRORS	CORRECTIONS
Vertical Trajectory Figure 6	a) Contact in front of face, elbows out, results in lifting motion straight up	1,2,3,4,5
	b) Feet parallel and even, so body extends straight up	1,2,3,4,5
	c) Body moves backwards on contact.	1,2,3,4,5
Very flat trajectory Figure 7	a) Athlete too far under ball so contact ball behind head resulting in a throwing motion forward.	1,2,3,4,5
	b) Athlete assumes over-exaggerated stride forward so no possible body extension upwards.	1,2,3,4,5
	c) Athlete too far behind ball, contact in front of sternum, results in 'chest' pass to target.	1,2,3,4,5
Ball spins through fingers Figure 8	a) Fingers too far apart.	1,2,3,4
	b) Too much conscious wrist extension and flexion.	1,2,3,4
	c) Contact with ball above head.	1,2,3,4
Ball bounces out of fingers	a) Fingers too firm	1,2
	b) Fingers and thumbs too close together.	6

1. Use video
    - show error
    - show correct technique

2. Re-do initial steps of forward progression

3. Use backward shaping

4. Footwork drills with athlete catching ball in correct volley position - coach can check base, body position, contact

5. Use flashcards
    - Athlete must raise contact point to be able to see card and communicate sign

6. Use weighted ball to overemphasize slight absorption of ball

DRILLS

These drills are designed to have the player move quickly to the correct position to pass the ball.

1. Volley ball forward, bounce, run to skip-stop, volley backward, bounce, continue.

2. Toss own ball away from self, run, skip-stop, volley into target 2-4m above floor.

3.

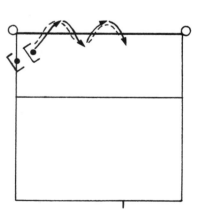

Figure 9

Each player has a ball;

Pass the ball over the net, duck under the net to receive and pass back over again;

Player moves down length of net.

4.

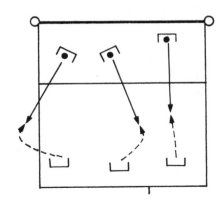

Figure 10

One ball for each pair;

One player with ball at net turns feet in direction of toss;

Partner reads feet and moves to the intended line of toss to skip-stop and volley ball up and back to tosser:

i)   Forward movement - partner starts on baseline.
ii) Backward movement - partner starts one step away from tosser.
iii) Lateral movement - partner starts at mid court.

5.

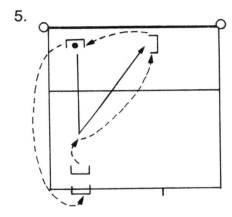

Figure 11

Group of four;

Tosser passes ball to back row player, indicating direction of pass with alignment of shoulers/feet;

Player moves to ball and passes to setter target;

Target catches and becomes new tosser, tosser goes to end of line, passer becomes new setter target.

These drills are designed to assist with the development of concentration and decision making.

1.

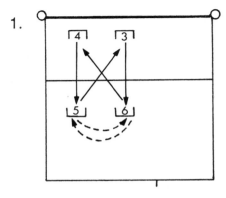

Figure 12

4 players, 2 balls;

Player 4 passes to 5 and 3 to 6; 5 and 6 volley cross-court; 4 and 3 catch; repeat;

Once the drill is moving smoothly;

i)   Players pass to exactly the same place, but 5 changes positions with 6.

ii) Both sets of players change positions after the volley; 4 with 3, and 5 with 6;

2.

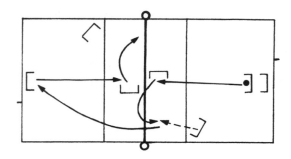

Figure 13

7 players, 1 ball;

Set up players in position 6, 3 and 4 on each side of net;

Position 6 passes to setter in 3, who sets attacker in 4 who volleys to opposite side position 6: only use volleys;

After contacting the ball, players move to the position they have just passed to and assume new role;

Note: Always start drill with two players at the ball.

3.

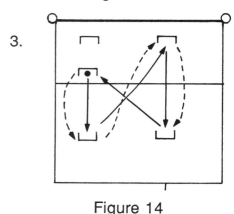

Figure 14

Set up five players, with one ball;

Volley straight ahead from net, volley cross-court from back court positions;

Players move to new position they have just volleyed to (follow the ball);

i)   add cartwheel ⎫
ii) 3 tuck jumps   ⎬ on way to new location
iii) add sprawl   ⎭

4.

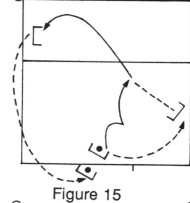

Figure 15

4 players, with two balls;

Player 6 bounces ball off floor, player 1 moves to set high cross-court set to target;

Follow the pass (target now becomes second tosser and tosser becomes player in #1, etc.);

* Can be used from all positions on court

5.

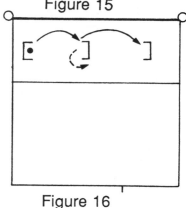

Figure 16

Three players, one ball;

Outside players volley to middle;

Middle player back volleys high in air to sideline and turns;

Continue, then rotate positions.

SUMMARY

- Players must move to the ball quickly and skip-stop to a staggered stance with the front foot pointing to the target. Balance is the key!

- The player's hips and shoulders should be square to the target.

- The cupped hands should be in position early, then move to contact the ball approximately 10cm from the eyes.

- The thumbs point back over the opposite ears, fingers spread.

- The player should utilize their entire body to add strength to the arms and hands, as they extend their knees and hips upward through the ball.

- For backward volleys move the pelvis forward slightly past the point of contact with the ball, just as the legs begin to push.

- The ball is contacted with the fleshy fingerpads.

- The follow through will assist in accuracy as the arms extend fully with the hands facing in the intended trajectory of the pass.

THE ATTACK

By: Larry Plennart
Keith Wasylik

THE ATTACK

A successful attack is the ultimate objective of a team's transition from serve reception or defence. The main objective of the attack itself is to direct the ball over the net in such a manner that the opposition will be unable to keep the ball in play, or unable to return it with an attack of their own.

The more reliance the attacker has that the attempted attack will be initiated from an ideal setting, the more the attacker can concentrate on a successful completion of the skill. The more variables that the attacker will have to contend with, such as an unexpected height or placement of the set, the more difficult the task becomes for the attacker to complete the transition sequence with an attack.

Upon completion of this unit, coaches will have a better understanding of:

- The approach and jumping action of the attack
- The hitting action of the spike
- The action of the tip

The fundamental attack described in this unit may be used in game situations to:

- Spike the ball into the opponent's court
- Tip the ball into the opponent's court

SKILL MECHANICS

While for teaching purposes the spike is readily broken down into the 'jumping action' and the 'hitting action', <u>the integration of the two into one continuous whole is as important as the learning of either part</u>. A good jump or good hitting action alone will not produce a good spike. The coach must appreciate that the sensation of spiking in mid-air is quite different from spiking while standing one the ground.

<u>READY POSITION</u>

Before the ball is set, all front row spikers should anticipate the spot where the setter would try to set the ball to. Typical sets might look as follows:

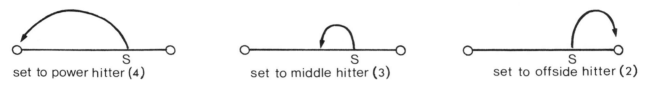

set to power hitter (4)   set to middle hitter (3)   set to offside hitter (2)

Figure 1: TYPICAL SETS

As soon as any blocking, digging or passing duties are completed, <u>the spikers must move to a position which allows them to approach the set</u>. Typical ready positions for these spike approaches would look as follows:

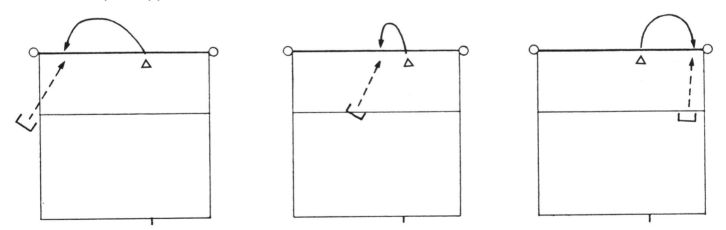

Figure 2: READY POSITIONS FOR RIGHT HANDED ATTACKERS

The ready positions should be 3-4 meters from the net for power and offside hitters, and 2-3 metres from the net for middle hitters. The knees are flexed and the body is approximately at a 45° angle to the net in #4 and #3. In position #2, the attacker waits with the body approximately parallel to the net.

THE APPROACH

The approach must carry the spiker to the exact spot the jump will be made (Figure 3).
It is important that the approach is flexible enough to permit some adjustment.

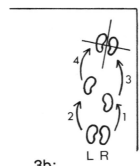

3a:
Right-handed spiker
in position 4 or 3

3b:
Right-handed spiker
in position 2

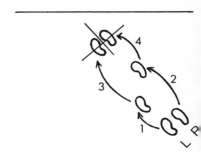

3c:
Left-handed spiker
in position 2

Figure 3: ATTACKER'S FOOTWORK

Steps 1 and 2 are orientation or adjustment steps for the body to be in a good location behind the ball. Steps 3 and 4 are the final preparation steps or closing steps prior to jumping. These final steps can be sequential or simultaneous as long as the forward foot does not land first. The feet are at an angle to the net with the foot opposite the hitting arm forward to allow for the shoulders to open and rotate slightly away from the ball. The weight of the body is on the middle part of the feet including the balls of the feet.

For a three step approach: use steps 2,3,4

For a two step approach: use steps 3 and 4

The approach would depend on location of the attacker's ready position, the location of the set and the movement skills of the attacker. The approach must also be timed so that the maximum height of the jump is realized at exactly the same time that the hitting action upon the ball occurs. The eyes should watch the set throughout the approach.

THE JUMP

The power of the jump is a culmination of several parts of the body exercising a force: the arms, by swinging from behind the spiker to in front of and above the shoulders, and the hips and knees by flexing and then extending.

The angles of the hips, knees and ankle joints are seen in Figure 4.

To ensure best possible height with best balance and control, the attacker should use a two-foot take-off. When landing, the attacker should land on both feet and flex the ankles, knees and hips to absorb body weight and maintain balance.

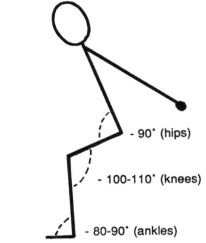

- 90° (hips)

- 100-110° (knees)

- 80-90° (ankles)

Figure 4: ATTACKER'S JUMPING ANGLES

THE HITTING ACTION

The ball should be struck from as high as possible, to allow for the best possible angle for the ball to go over the net, past blockers' hands, and in the court. Thus the ball should ultimately be contacted with a full extension of the hitting arm above and slightly in front of the shoulder. A powerful spike is achieved by a prestretching of the muscles involved. The arm swing in the jumping action brings both arms to their initial position in front of the spiker; either straight or bent and just above the head (Figure 5a). From this position, the elbow of the hitting arm is drawn back, as though drawing a bow string from the non-hitting hand to the side of the head (Figure 5b). The hand continues its backward direction, above and slightly behind the head. The elbow of the non-hitting arm begins its forward motion and the elbow of the hitting arm beings its upward and forward action towards the ball with the relaxed forearm whipping up towards the ball (Figure 5c). Finally, the hitting hand is snapped onto the ball directly above the elbow, by the force of the hip flextion, shoulder rotation and elevation, the tricep pull, and the wrist snap (Figure 5d).

Figure 5: HITTING ACTION

The ball should be struck with an open hand, with the fingers slightly apart and slightly bent. The palm of the hand strikes the ball first, followed immediately by the fingers which are brought into contact with the ball by the final wrist snap.

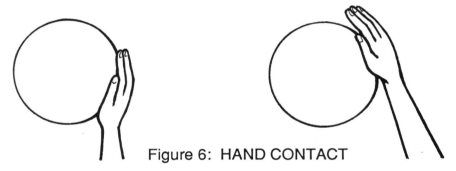

Figure 6: HAND CONTACT

CONTROLLING TRAJECTORY

Because of the angled approach to the ball and the angled take-off while jumping, a natural swing and follow-through (for right-handed attackers in positions #4 and #3, and left-handed in #2) will result in a 'cross-court' attack. (Refer to Figures 3a and 3b.)

A second target for attackers should be to hit 'down the line' or 'cut back' for middle players (Figure 7).

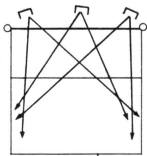

Figure 7: TWO TARGET AREAS FOR ATTACKERS

Two methods of effecting a line attack are:

Adjust the final foot placement for jumping (Figure 8). Change the final two steps of the approach to face the ball and the line target.

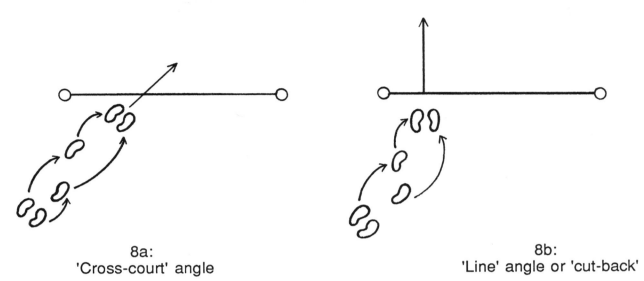

8a:
'Cross-court' angle

8b:
'Line' angle or 'cut-back'

Figure 8: FOOTWORK FOR DIFFERENT ATTACK ANGLES

Adjust the non-hitting arm swing (elbow) to move out and down instead of forward and down (Figure 9).

9a:
'Cross-court' shot

9b:
'Line' shot or 'cut-back'

Figure 9: FRONT VIEW OF NON-HITTING ELBOW ACTION

This added stretch across the front of the shoulders will aid in bringing the hitting elbow up and across the body to attack the line.

THE TIP

Any off-speed attack should follow through exactly the same approach and arm action as described above, except for the final contact phase of the hand. In the tip, the hand is not allowed to snap into the ball; rather the tip becomes a softly tapped ball with the fingers. The contact by the fingers should be on the ball where the palm would have contacted in the spike. The contact is similar to volleying with one hand and can force the ball up (Figure 10), forward or down.

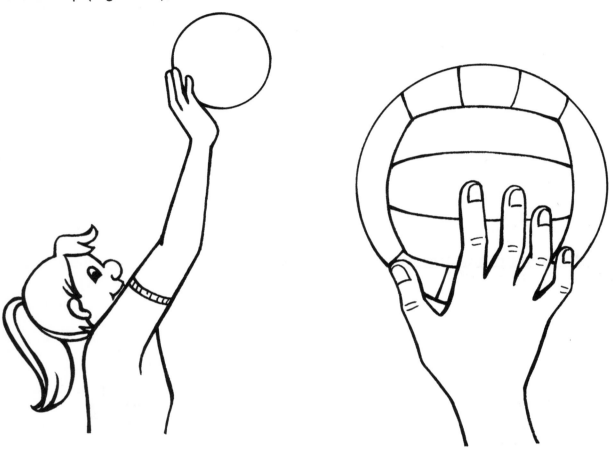

Figure 10: THE TIP (UPWARD AND OVER A BLOCK)

The tip should be used as an offensive weapon which changes the nature of the anticipated attack by the defence. It should exploit openings in the defensive alignment of the opposing team. It can also be used to keep a poorly set ball in play when an attempted spike's possiblity of success is minimal. Consistency is the key to success for this skill: consistent approach, jump and timing with the contact of the ball to simulate spike timing.

TEACHING PROGRESSION

These drills are designed to assist in learning the correct footwork for the attack.

Drill 1

- All players in 3 lines away from net. Left handed players angled away from right handed players.

- Coach demonstrates and walks players through L and R approach.

- Emphasize acceleration to the correct spot with balance and proper closing steps.

Drill 2

- Add arm swing and jump to approach.

Drill 3

- Add relaxed hitting motion for approach and jump.

- Emphasize hitting at the top of the jump and landing on balance facing the direction of the intended attack.

Drill 4

- Practice
  - at various speeds
  - at various angles to net in player positions
  - with movement after simulated serve reception or defence, etc.

Drill 5

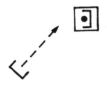

Figure 12

- partners, one ball

a) partner stands on chair and holds ball up. Attacker approaches and jumps to touch ball with two hands at top of jump.

b) Partner tosses ball approximately 4m high. Attacker approaches and catches ball with two hands at top of jump.

The following drills are designed to assist in learning the correct arm action and hand contact for the attack.

Drill 6

Figure 13

a) Spike

- Each player has a ball. Similar to underhand serve.

- Small toss with non-hitting hand. Swing hitting arm under ball to full extension and snap wrist to drive ball with spin straight up into air.

b) Tip

- Self toss and volley with one hand into target.

Drill 7

Figure 14

- Partners using tennis balls, mini footballs, shuttlecocks.

- Practice throwing with proper shoulder rotation and elevation.

- Emphasize elbow moving up and foward.

- Wrist snap so fingers follow direction of ball.

Drill 8

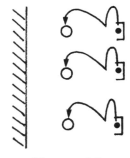

Figure 15

- Each player has a ball.

a) Short self toss and using correct arm action spike ball against wall. Snap wrist.

Emphasize correct arm action so ball travels parallel to the ground and with topspin.

b) Short self toss and using correct arm action swing and tip ball into bucket, 1/2 way to wall.

Drill 9

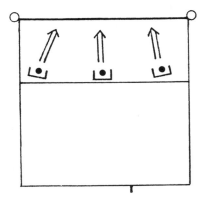

Figure 16

- Players 2-3m from net.
- Self toss and standing spike over the net, cross court.

Drill 10

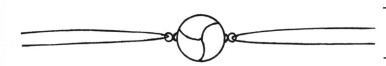

Figure 17

- Use stationary ball, attached by elastic cords to supports.

- Players approach jump and spike ball.

Drill 11

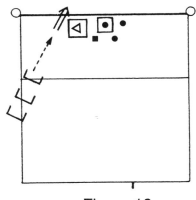

Figure 18

- Group of 3 or 4 players

- Coach on chair or table approximately 1-2m away from net.

- Coach holds ball in one hand.

- Players approach, jump and spike ball out of coach's hand (over the net).

- Coach should vary height for each player to emphasize maximum reach and extension.

COMMON FAULTS, ERRORS AND CORRECTIONS
(ASSUMING CONSISTENT SETS)

COMMON FAULTS	ERRORS	CORRECTIONS

Erratic contacts	a) Inconsistent approach
	  - no approach
	  - incorrect footwork
		1,2

	b) Poor eye-hand coordination	3,4
Incorrect ball trajectory		
- Too high	a) Incorrect foot position on jump	1,2,5
	b) Poor timing	1,3,5,6
	c) Firm hand or fist for contact	3,5,6

- Too low
  (into net or
   block, etc.)
	a) Incorrect position on jump	1,2,5

	b) Poor timing	1,3,5,6
	c) Elbow leading down not up	3,5,6
- Too wide	a) Incorrect foot position	1,5,6
	b) Armswing too slow	5,6
No top spin	a) Contact with heel of hand - fingers don't catch up to ball	4,5,6
	b) Contact with fist or firm hand	5,6,7
Lack of power	a) Erratic or no approach	1,2,5,6
	b) Incorrect sequence of body parts	1,5,6,7
Touching the net	a) Set too close	8,9
	b) Arm follows through too far	5,8,9
Carried ball on tip	a) Loose wrist	3,5,6,10
	b) Open palm	3,5,6,10
	c) Inconsistent contacts	1,4,5,6

CORRECTIONS:

1. Work on approach pattern on floor without ball (i.e. "dance" steps).
2. Mark starting point for approach. Player must return each time.
3. Striking and tapping game.
4. Vision check.
5. Use video.
6. Re-do progressions.
7. Flexibility exercises.
8. Toss close sets, <u>no</u> block, attacker stops follow through.
9. Setter practices setting 1/2 to 1m off the net.
10. Strength exercises.

DRILLS

The following drills are designed to improve the consistency of the timing and effectiveness of the attack.

Drill 1

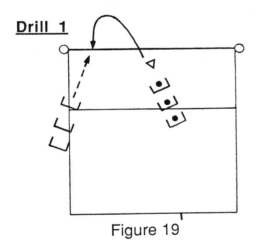

Figure 19

- Line of attackers.

- Line of feeders with a ball each beside coach.

- Coach tosses medium high set for attackers to approach and spike.

- After spike, shag ball and join the feeder line.

Drill 2

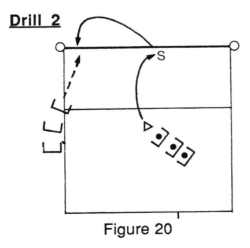

Figure 20

- Add setter to previous drill.

- Coach now tosses to setter.

- Setter must give consistent sets.

Drill 3

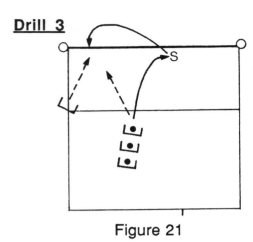

Figure 21

- Line of attackers, each with a ball, except first spiker.

- Second person in line tosses ball to setter (from in court) and move to cover.

- Then move outside to become attacker

Drill 4

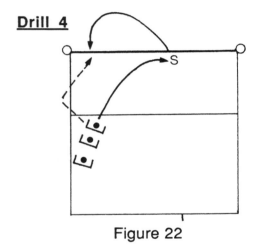

Figure 22

- Attackers in line each with a ball.

- First player tosses ball to setter, then moves outside court to approach and spike.

- Shag ball and return.

Drill 5

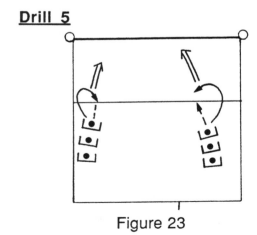

Figure 23

- Two lines of attackers, each with a ball.

- Players toss high sets for themselves and approach and spike cross-court from 3m line.

Drill 6

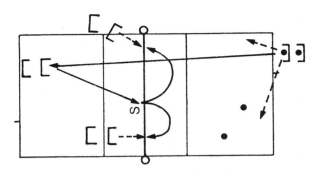

Figure 24

- 2 players serving.
- 2 players receiving serve.
- 2 setters alternate setting.
- 2 pairs of players (4) attacking.
- 2 players shagging (or physical training).

- One player serves, then moves to one side of court.

- Receivers pass the serve to setter; setter sets normal outside set.

- Attackers spike/tip ball away from/to server in new position.

- Rotate after 2 minutes.

Drill 7

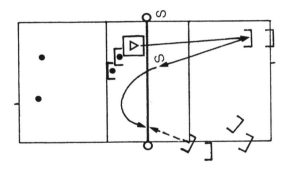

Figure 25

- 2 players feeding balls to coach.
- 2 pairs of players (4) digging attacks.
- 2 setters alternating.
- 2 attackers.
- 2 shaggers.

- Coach spikes/tips ball at defenders

- Dig, set, spike

- Players move to cover

- After 2-3 minutes, switch positions.

Drill 8

- Groups of 3, one ball.

- One attacker vs 2 blockers with hands up in blocking position.

- Attacker self tosses and one blocker drops hands.

- Attacker spikes ball over head of blocker who dropped hands.

Drill 9

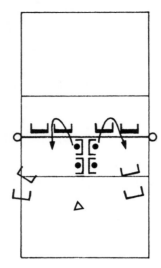

Figure 26

- Groups of six.

- 2 players toss or set, 2 players attack alternately, 2 players block about 1m apart.

- Coach signals whether one block, double block, no block.

- Attackers must attack open space.

- After 4-5 minutes switch.

HINTS: -   Work for consistent but accelerating approach to the ball.

-   Have attackers attack to/away from targets.

-   Add transition movements to attack: from serve reception, defence, add cover, etc.

SUMMARY

- Assume the ready position, 3-4m from the net.
- The approach must:
  - Carry the attacker to the correct take-off position.
  - Transfer horizontal force into jumping power.
  - Terminate with the correct foot touching the floor last.
  - Terminate at the correct time for the jump.
  - Terminate with a 2-foot jump.
- The jump is accomplished through the lifting of the arms and the thrust of the legs.
- The hitting action of the spike is accomplished through:
  - Both arms swinging up in front of the body to full extension.
  - Drawing the hitting elbow back.
  - Leading the swing with the non-hitting elbow moving forward
  - Whipping the elbow of the hitting arm upwards to the ball.
  - Snapping the wrist, with an open hand, onto the ball.
- The tip is initiated with exactly the same approach and jumping action. However, the ball is tapped with the fingers to desired area.
- Landing should be flexed and on balance.

THE BLOCK

By: Brad Kilb
Keith Wasylik

THE BLOCK

Effective blocking is the key to good team defence. Some coaches consider good aggressive blocking as the biggest psycho - logical weapon an individual player or team has in their arsenal. To be able to "shut down" the opponent's attack and force them into a secondary game plan is certainly an important factor in success.

On completion of this unit, the coach will have a better understanding of:

- The body mechanics of the block

- The different types of blocks

- How to position the block

- How to time the block

The skill of blocking in various game situations is used to:

- Stop the opponent's attack from crossing the net

- Re-direct the opponent's attack to a well-defended part of the court.

SKILL MECHANICS

READY POSITION

The player should stand with their feet perpendicular to the centre line and about 20-30cm back from the line. Feet should be shoulder width apart. The back is straight, and hands are held above and slightly in front of the shoulders. Hands of middle blockers are held higher.

Figure 1: READY POSITION

TAKE-OFF

Players should try to move laterally to desired position and then jump straight up rather than floating across the net. Knees are bent then extend fully thrusting with the knees and ankles. The back remains straight. The arms do not swing, but remain above the shoulders throughout.

UPPER BODY ACTION

The hands move from the shoulders directly above the net. It is important that the hands remain in front of the shoulders throughout and reach as high as possible, as quickly as possible. The arms are fully extended with the elbows locked. The wrists are firm, with the fingers spread in the shape of the ball. The hands are held just far enough apart to stop a ball from passing through (Figure 2). Just prior to contact with the ball, the abdominal muscles tighten and the shoulders shrug to give added strength. The head is tilted back slightly to allow the eyes a good view of the ball and the spiking action.

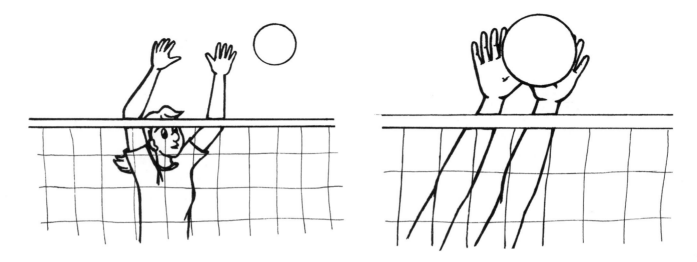

Figure 2: CONTACT WITH THE BALL

LANDING

After contact with the ball, the hands are withdrawn to avoid a net foul. The player should absorb the shock of landing by flexing the ankles, knees and hips upon landing. A balanced landing is important so that the next action may be accomplished, such as preparing for the transition to offence.

TYPES OF BLOCKS

SOFT BLOCK

The soft block or defensive block is utilized by players who are not able to get their hands above the height of the net. This may occur due to the lack of height/jump of the player, a late block or an out-of-position block. In the soft block, the player places the palms of their hands up to form a <u>rebounding surface for the ball</u> (Figure 3). The player should jump a little further back from the net to intercept the trajectory of the ball. Although this block appears simple, the timing and placement of the hands is extremely difficult. The ball can rebound deep into the opponents court, or up to their own teammates; <u>the concept is to defend court area</u>!

Figure 3: SOFT BLOCK

ATTACK BLOCK

For this offensive block the player <u>penetrates with their hands angled above the opponent's court</u>, resulting in a "roof" over the ball. As the attacker spikes the ball, the ball rebounds down towards the floor. This block is easy to position, since the blocker's hands are usually close to the ball. Coaches must emphasize that the "attack block" or "stuff" or "slam" gets its names from the "roof position" and <u>not</u> from swinging the arms at the ball (Figure 4).

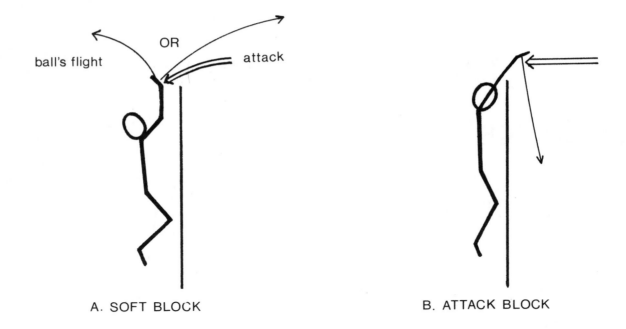

Figure 4: TWO TYPES OF BLOCKS

POSITIONING

Obviously, the best blocking form is of little use unless the block is placed in a position to intercept the spiker. It is important to emphasize that the block must be <u>positioned according to where the ball crosses the net, and not where the attacker contacts the ball</u>. A common blocking procedure would be:

1) Watch the setter - to determine the direction of the set.

2) Watch the set - to determine trajectory and final destination.

3) Watch the attacker's feet - try to position the take-off point opposite the direction of the attacker's feet.

4) Watch the attacker's arms - for signals of direction and speed of attack.

5) Put your hands on the ball

6) The inside hand of the blocker should be where the ball is going to cross the net and the outside hand turned in slightly toward the court.

TIMING THE BLOCK

Knowing when to jump for blocking will depend upon the type of attack, and the characteristics of each individual attacker. A basic rule is that the blocker should <u>jump just after the attacker on most sets</u>. To block quick attacks, the blocker should <u>jump at the same time as the set</u>. (Remember the high starting position of the hands). The other factor to consider with timing the block is the position of the attacker relative to the distance off the net. <u>For a ball set back near the attack line, a blocker might wait until the attacker begins the spiking arm action, before jumping</u>. The deeper the set, the longer the blocker should wait.

TEACHING PROGRESSION

These drills are designed to introduce basic blocking technique.

Drill 1

- partners facing each other, one ball.
- one player starts in ready position for blocking.
- partners toss ball and spike parallel to ground over blocker's head.
- blocker must time correct body extension and hand placement to block ball (soft or attack).
- switch after 6

Drill 2

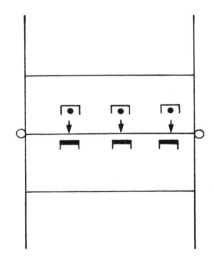

- partners, one ball, attacker up on chair.

  a) - attacker holds ball
     - blocker jumps and puts palms on ball (soft or attack).

  b) - attacker tosses and spikes ball into block as blocker times jump to stop ball (soft or attack).
     - adjust the net height if necessary.

Drill 3

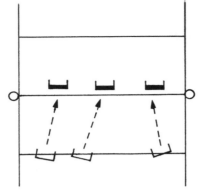

- partners, attacker now approaches straight from 3-4m away.

    a) jump and mime spike action (no ball).

    b) jump and throw ball into block (execute soft or attack block).

Drill 4

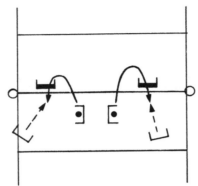

- group of 3, one ball.

- player tosses medium hight sets, attacker approaches and spikes into block.

    * soft block or attack if possible.
    * keep ball off net slightly to avoid collisions and injuries.

COMMON FAULTS, ERRORS AND CORRECTIONS

FAULTS	ERRORS	CORRECTIONS
Touching the net	a) Jumping too close to the net	1,2,3,4
	b) Swinging the arms	1,3,5
	c) 'Piking' at the hips	1,3,4
Ball in between body and net	a) Jumping too high with arms straight up	1,3,5
	b) Jumping too far off net	2,3
Inconsistent or no contact with ball	a) Eyes closed	1,3
	b) Moving arms or hands	1,3,5

FAULTS	ERRORS	CORRECTIONS
	c) 'Soft' hands	3 (Emphasize firm wrists and hands)
	d) Jumping too high (i.e. forearms and elbows exposed)	1,3,5
	e) Inconsistent spikers	6

CORRECTIONS

1) Use mirror or video for correct posture while jumping
2) Move foot placement
3) Re-do teaching progression
4) Coach physically holds blocker off net during jump
5) Use lower net and higher hands
6) Do not attempt to block

DRILLS

The following drills are designed to aid the development of proper positioning:

Drill 1

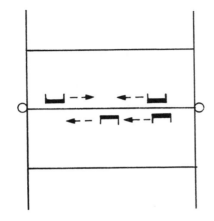

- blockers at net (or line)

- work on footwork patterns of moving 1,2 or 3 steps (see movement section)

Drill 2

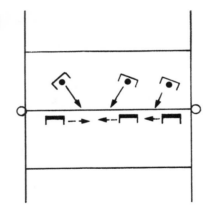

- partners, one ball, attacker up on chair

- attacker turns feet to indicate direction of approach

- blocker moves over to correct position

    a) attacker throws ball into block as blocker jumps

    b) attacker tosses and spikes ball into block

Drill 3

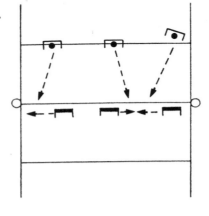

- partners, one ball, attacker approaches the net at different angles (stay off net)

    a) jump and throw ball (along approach line) into block

    b) toss, jump and spike along approach line

Drill 4

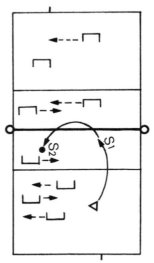

- team spaced apart on 1/2 court, one ball

a) - coach tosses ball to setter, setter sets different trajectory sets forward

    - blockers move parallel to net to spot where the trajectory of the ball intersects the net

    - second setter returns ball to coach

b) - use other 1/2 of court and back sets

c) - players call out where ball is going - front, back, high, inside, etc.

The following drills are designed to assist with the development of proper position and the timing of the block:

Drill 5

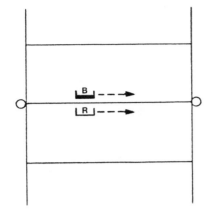

- partners, R is the 'Rabbit' (attacker)

- R moves anywhere along the net, jumps and places one fist above the net

- the blocker B must follow the 'rabbit' and after the attacker jumps to place a fist above the net, the blocker must try to surround that fist with both hands

- agree on 5-10 good blocks, rest while other groups work, then switch

* jump <u>after</u> the attacker ('rabbit') jumps

Drill 6

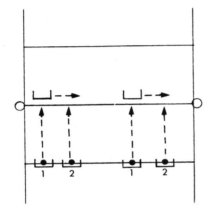

- groups of 3, two balls

- attacker 1 approaches, then attacker 2 approaches

- blocker blocks first attack, then moves over to stop second attack

   a) attackers jump and throw ball into block

   b) attackers toss, jump and spike ball into block

Drill 7

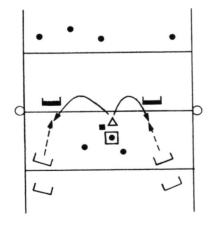

- coach tosses balls to correct attack zones

- attackers approach and jump and spike along approach line

- blockers must position themselves correctly and time jump to block

- switch after 5

Drill 8

a) - same as previous drill
   - coach tosses to setter who sets attackers

b) - if opponents use middle attacks then add a line of attackers in position #3 and a middle blocker opposite.

SUMMARY

- The ready position is close to the net, with hands above the shoulders or higher for middle blockers

- The take-off is initiated with good knee flexion and extension

- The hands thrust up and over the net as soon as possible

- On contact with the ball: tighten abdominal muscles, locked elbows, firm wrists, head back slightly, eyes on the ball

- The fingers are spread to cover as large an area as possible

- The landing is controlled and balanced

- Players should be able to execute two types of blocks:

  - Soft block (defensive)
  - Attack block (aggressive)

- The blocker should watch the set and then the attacker's foot position to determine the direction of the attack

- The blocker should jump just after the attacker for most sets and at the same time as the set for quick sets

THE SERVE

By Keith Wasylik

THE SERVE

Serving is the action that starts play in a volleyball game and a team's first opportunity to score a point. A consistent, well placed serve can also lead to inaccurate passes by the opponents and the possibility of the serving team having to defend an easy attack.

Consistency is the foundation of good serving. Good serving is one of the key steps leading to good team defence. Upon completion of this section, coaches will have a better understanding of:

- The mechanics of the basic serves

    - Underhand

    - Sidearm

    - Overhand

UNDERHAND SERVE

GETTING READY

- Establish a target line that goes past the toes towards the serving target.

- Stand with knees bent and with the feet <u>less</u> than shoulder width apart.

- The feet should be at approximately a 35°-40° angle to the target line.

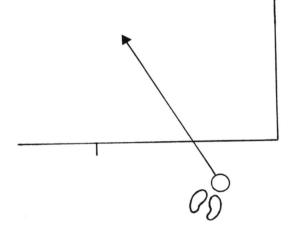

- Hold the ball in the fingers of the non-striking hand, over the target line, in front of the striking arm and shoulder, and about mid-thigh height.

- Look at the target, then look at the ball.

Figure 1: GETTING READY
(Ball and foot placement for a right-handed server serving cross-court)

BODY MOVEMENT (Figure 2)

- Draw the striking arm straight back.

- <u>Step with the forward foot</u> so it points in the direction of the intended target, <u>and swing forward.</u>

- The fingers of the support hand should release the ball rather than toss it in the air.

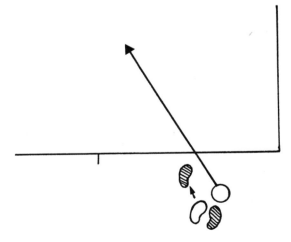

Figure 2: BODY MOVEMENT

CONTACT

- The striking hand can be a fist, 1/2 fist open.

- The server should aim to contact the ball at a spot on the back of the ball directly opposite the intended line of flight (i.e. a higher trajectory serve requires a contact closer to the bottom of the ball).

- The server should aim to contact the ball with the <u>middle of the palm</u> of the hand.

- The arm should follow-through in the intended direction of the serve.

SIDEARM SERVE

<u>GETTING READY</u> (Figure 3)

- Establish a target line past the toes towards the serving target.

- Stand with knees bent and with the feet <u>less than shoulders width apart</u>.

- The feet should be at a 90° angle to the target line.

- Hold the ball in the fingers of the non-striking hand, with a slightly bent elbow and shoulder-high in the mid-line of the body.

- Look at the target, then look at the ball.

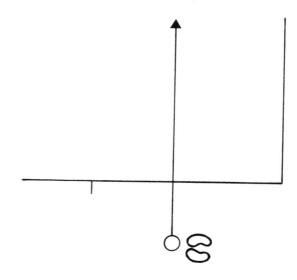

Figure 3: GETTING READY
(Ball and foot placement for a left-handed server serving down the line)

BODY MOVEMENT

- Draw the striking hand back slightly.

- Step with the forward foot so it opens <u>slightly</u> to the target <u>and</u> swing forward towards the top of the net.

- Keep the forward knee bent.

- The fingers of the support hand should release the ball.

CONTACT

- The striking hand and contact surface are identical to the underhand serve.
- The server should aim to contact the ball at a spot on the back of the ball directly opposite the intended line of flight.

- The arm should follow-through in the direction of the serve.

OVERHAND SERVE

GETTING READY

- Establish a target line.

- Stand with the knees bent and with the feet <u>shoulder width apart or less</u>.

- The feet should be at approximately a 35°-45° angle to the target line.

- Hold the ball in the fingers of the non-striking hand, over the target line, about shoulder height.

- Both arms are bent slightly and comfortable.

- The fingers of the striking hand REST lightly on the top of the ball pointing at the target. The elbow should be high so that the forearm is parallel to the ground.

- Look at the target, then look at the ball.

Figure 4: GETTING READY

BODY MOVEMENT

- Gently lift the ball straight up in the air (the fingers actually drop away from the ball) to a point at or slightly above the server's reach. The toss must be accurate.

- Simultaneously either a) draw the elbow back and high (similar to a "bow and arrow")

  OR

  b) draw the hand back behind the hitting shoulder, keep the elbow high (similar to a "beginning" tennis serve).

- <u>Step with the forward foot</u> so it points in the direction of the serving target, <u>and swing up and forward</u> to contact the ball.

- Keep the forward knee bent as long as possible.

CONTACT

- Identical to the other two serves mentioned.

TEACHING PROGRESSION

The following drills are designed to develop consistent serving technique:

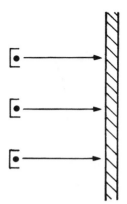

1. Players each have a ball.

   Serve ball against the wall.

   Coach gives feedback on style/technique.

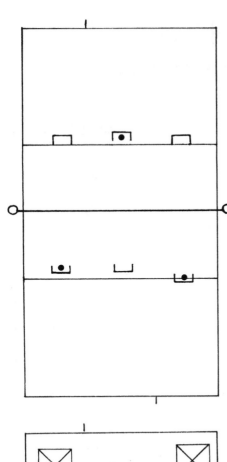

2. Partners with one ball.

   Players serve to each across net, approximately 3m from net.

   Coach gives feedback on technique.

3. Same as drill #2.

   Each time partners complete two 'good' serves, back up 1m.

   Try to finish past the baseline.

4. Same as drill #2.

   Coach video tapes server; shows form; makes corrections; practice form.

5. Same as drill #3.

   Receiving partner moves to new location on court.

   Server must adjust target line, body movement and contact to serve to new target.

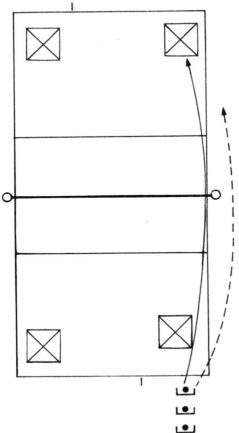

6. Players each have a ball.

   Four mats on courts for serving targets.

   Player serves at specific target, then sprints around to other side to shag ball.

   Server then joins other line.

   Coaches should use appropriate serving line for group (i.e. 6m back from the net may be correct in some cases).

COMMON FAULTS, ERRORS
AND CORRECTIONS

FAULT	ERROR	CORRECTIONS
Incorrect trajectory - left	a) Poor toss left b) Step is in that direction c) Contact on side of ball	1,2,3 2,3,4 1,2,3,5
- right	a) Poor toss right b) Step is in that direction c) Contact on side of ball	1,2,3 1,2,3,4 1,2,3,5
- too high	a) Poor toss behind b) Step too long, past ball c) Contact on bottom of ball	1,2,3 2,3,4,5 1,3,5
- too low	a) Poor toss forward b) Step too short c) Contact on top of ball d) Front knee straightens	1,2,3 3,4,5 1,3,5 2,3,4
Ball goes too far	a) Trajectory too high b) Player swings too hard	(see above) 6,7,8
Ball never goes far enough	a) Trajectory too low b) Improper sequence of body parts c) Lack of strength	(see above) 2,3,4,5,6 3,4,9,10,11

CORRECTION

1) Practice toss
2) Use mirror
3) Use video
4) Draw foot pattern on floor
5) Use stationary ball, check the eyes
6) Shorter backswing
7) Move player back
8) Wider stance and no step
9) Move player closer
10) Narrower stance, to force step or two steps
11) Strength training

SUMMARY

- Establish a target line

- Knees bent and feet shoulder width apart or less

- Tee-up the ball in the support hand

- Look at the target, then the ball

- Step and swing

- Contact is made with the middle of the palm on the back of the ball directly opposite the intended trajectory

- The hand and arms should follow through the ball towards the target

BASIC TEAM TACTICS

By   Keith Wasylik

BASIC TEAM TACTICS

Along with the development and acquisition of basic skills, the coach must introduce the players to the concepts of volleyball team play. The dual objective of the game of volleyball is to 1) get the ball over the net and down on the opponent's court, and 2) prevent the ball from landing on your own court.

Upon completion of this section, the coach will have a better understanding of:

- The basis of volleyball team systems

- The basic principles of serve reception and possible applications

- The basic principles of attack coverage and possible applications

- The basic principles of defence against an attack and against a free ball and possible applications

The key phrase for this section is:

"Quality within simplicity"

CYCLE OF ACTIONS
IN VOLLEYBALL

Although founded on specific individual skills, the nature of the game of volleyball is cyclical, given the fact that one successful action is simply a connection in a sequence of actions that may follow or be repeated (Figure1).

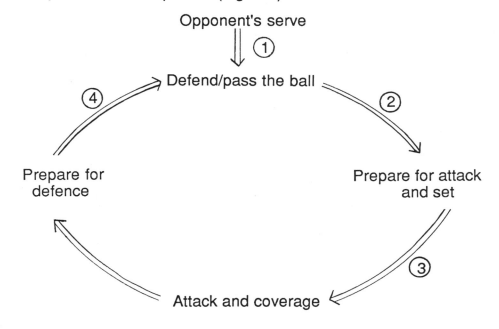

Figure 1: CYCLE OF VOLLEYBALL ACTIONS

The arrows indicate changes in individual player movements and shifts in team patterns to allow for the completion of the cycle. Before each of the indicated steps of the cycle, some tasks must be accomplished by the players. Here is an example for each step:

Step 1: Call the ball

Step 2: Setter - while moving into position, should look at blockers/defenders for cues to best choice of sets.

Step 3: Attackers - should look at blockers/defenders for cues to best attack choice.

Step 4: Blockers/defenders - watch setter and attackers for cues to direction of set and direction and type of attack.

Obviously while one team is preparing to attack, their opponents are preparing to defend. Yet many coaches fail to teach the cues necessary to make either preparation effective. Players should see themselves as participants in a live video or computer game: constantly checking for new information and monitoring the situation.

Besides the individual skills and static starting patterns of team play, coaches must work on the transition from one phase of the volleyball cycle to the next.

TERMINOLOGY

Common volleyball systems are either unspecialized or specialized. In a specialized system, specific roles are given to some or all players. For example, one or two players can be assigned setting duties for all or most situations. Also, the other players can be assigned a prioritized position from which to attack or defend. As for an unspecialized system, all players will be called upon to fill every role. In such a system, the tasks assigned to a specific position on the court (e.g. player in position 3 is the setter) will be that of the player at this position, according to order of rotation.

When using a numerical terminology to identify a volleyball system, most people will refer to the number of players assigned at hitting and setting. If we respect this basic principle, the following terminology would apply:

6-6:   Unspecialized system; all players will hit or set, depending on rotation

4-2:   Specialized system where four players are assigned to hitting and two players set; this involves use of a front row player as setter in all situations.

6-2:   Specialized system where all players will hit but only two will be setting; this involves use of a back row player as setter in all situations.

5-1:   Specialized system where five players will hit but only one player will set; this involves use of the same player as setter, whether he/she is in the front row or back row.

In this article, we will be using a front row setter when giving examples or application of the principles of team tactics . But we will look at variations involving unspecialized and specialized systems.

SERVE RECEPTION TO ATTACK

PRINCIPLES

Primary Tasks

- cover the court
  - angled and facing the server
- pass the ball to the designated target area
  - move and face the ball and target

Secondary Tasks

- set and cover
- attack

Guidelines

- initial position
  - every player should participate, except setter
  - players must be in their correct rotational order at the time of serve (Figure 2)
  - dead angles are not covered by initial position
  - players play in two clear and related rows: front and back
  - players in the same row are equidistant from the server and angled to face the server
  - back row players are in the middle of the angle created by the front row players

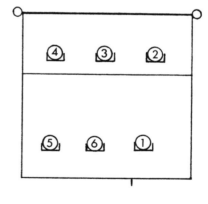

Figure 2

- passing the ball
  - players verbally indicate commitment to play the ball
  - players 'open up' to the passer
  - movement is frontwards (forward or 45°), not sideways
  - movement back should be limited to one step
  - trajectory of the pass is dictated by the location of the passing target and the number and location of the attackers

SERVE RECEPTION PATTERNS

An effective team pattern for covering the court with 5 players receiving is the W formation (Figure 3).

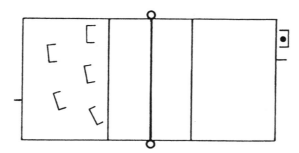

Figure 3: THE 'W' FORMATION

Against a strong serving team, move the entire W closer to the baseline. Against a weak serving team, move the W closer to the attack line.

The players should be facing the server with their feet slightly staggered and in a comfortable position.

Another effective pattern using 5 players to receive is the M formation (Figure 4). This could be used against teams with very deep, hard serves.

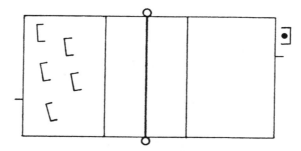

Figure 4: THE 'M' FORMATION

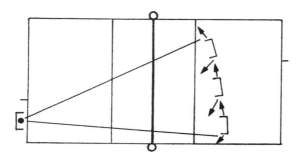
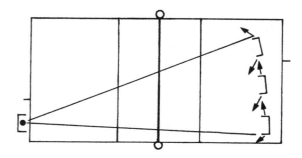

Figure 5: RECEIVERS EQUIDISTANCE FROM SERVER

USING AN UNSPECIALIZED SYSTEM

With a five player pattern, the sixth position can now be designated as the passing target/setting position (Figure 6).

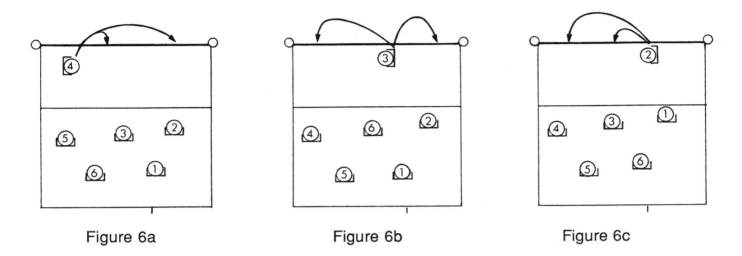

Figure 6a   Figure 6b   Figure 6c

Figure 6: PASSING TARGETS AND SETTER

The location in Figure 6a might prove effective if all of your players are left handed. If you wish to spread out your attackers, Figure 6b would be more appropriate. To utilize a middle attack over a short middle blocker, Figure 6c would be a good choice.

* Assuming a 2 attacker system with a middle front (#3) passing target/setter, in this unspecialized system, whoever rotates into position #3 would be the setter and whoever is in positions #4 and #2 would be the hitters.

Attack Coverage

- follow or collapse to the ball (Figure 7)
- split to a low position and face the block

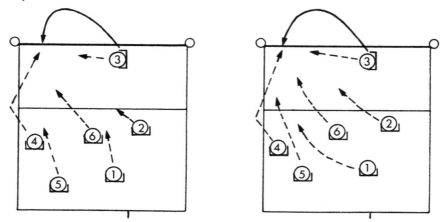

Figure 7: SERVE RECEPTION PATTERN TO ATTACK COVERAGE

The idea is to cover two zones around the block: short and deep. With a poor block you only need one or two people up short. Against a strong tall block a team could use 3 people up close to cover their attackers.

USING A SPECIALIZED SYSTEM

Good passing should allow you to get your best setter to the target area and your attackers to attack from advantageous court positions.

- Goals
    - Want your two best athletes (movement and volley) setting the ball
    - Want your strongest attackers hitting from positions #4 and #3 (because other team has short middle block). (Figure 8)
- Using a front court setter, a team's offense might look like this:

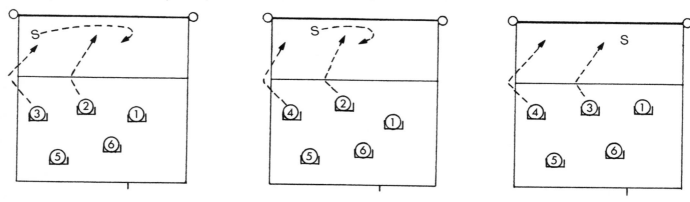

Figure 8: SETTER MOVES TO PASSING TARGET

If you wish to specialize further you might try to balance the offensive strength of your rotation (Figure 9).

This would let P1 and P2 each attack from #4, two out of three rotations on serve reception. In the third rotation, they could switch places and go to #4 <u>after</u> your team has attacked the ball to the other side of the net.

When one setter rotates to the back row, the second setter (opposite in rotation) would rotate to the front court to do the setting.

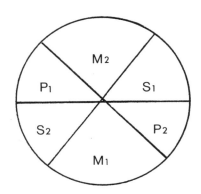

S1 = Best Setter
S2 = Second Setter
M1 = Best Middle H.
M2 = Second Middle H.
P1 = Best Power H.
P2 = Second Power H.

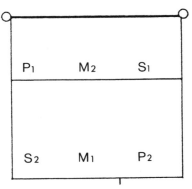

Figure 9: ROTATION ORDER

Attack Coverage

- follow or collapse to the back (Figure 10)
- split to a low position and face the block

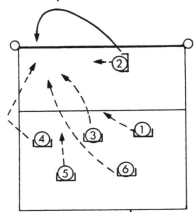
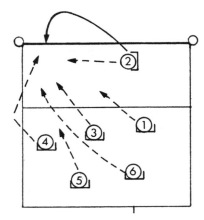

Figure 10: ATTACK COVERAGE WITH SPECIALIZED FRONT COURT SETTER

* This allows the spikers and setters to keep their court relationship and prepares 6 for a defensive position.

DEFENCE TO ATTACK

PRINCIPLES

Primary Tasks

- prevent the ball from hitting the court
  - at the net
  - back court

Secondary Tasks

- set and cover
- attack

Guidelines

- initial position
  - every player participates
  - blockers at the net, inside attackers
    - how many blockers required: none or one?
  - back court players in specified positions depending on opponent's skills
    - middle back (#6) player: up or back?
  - protecting the court
    - establish good court position
    - establish good body position
    - contact the ball

DEFENCE PATTERNS ON ATTACK

6-up Defence

The name of this system refers to the middle back (position #6) player starting in a defensive position in the middle of the court near the attack line. Defence against:

- weak attacking teams

- teams that tip frequently

The player with the best recovery skills should be placed in #6, because this position should be contacting many balls. The other defenders are placed around the 'shadow' of the block. (Remember a bad block is worse than no block.) (Figure 13)

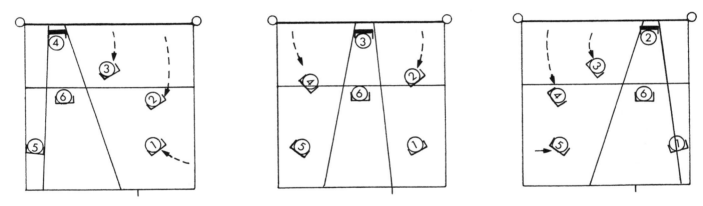

Figure 13: 6-UP DEFENCE WITH ONE BLOCKER

6-Back Defence

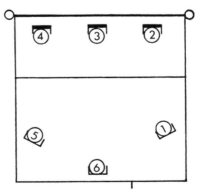

This system places the player in middle back (position #6) in a starting defensive position near the baseline (Figure 14).

Figure 14: STARTING POSITIONS FOR A '6-BACK' DEFENCE

The player in #6 should be good at reading the approach and intention of the opposing attackers. This is a good defence against:

- strong consistent attacking teams
- teams that rarely tip short

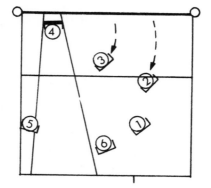 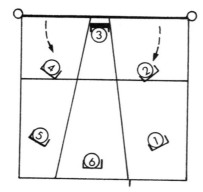 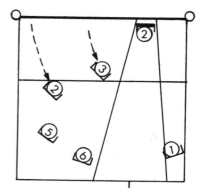

Figure 15: '6-BACK' DEFENCE WITH ONE BLOCKER

Variation:

Instead of player #6 shifting cross-court from the attacker (and one of the front court players covering tips) a coach might have #6 shift down the line from the attacker (and a back court player could cover tips). (Figure 16)

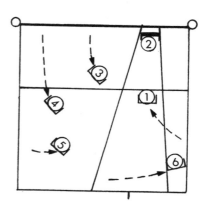

Figure 16: '6-BACK' DEFENCE VARIATION

DEFENCE PATTERN ON FREE BALL

Shortly after the second contact by the opponents, a team should be able to recognize whether or not the ball will be attacked. If not, the front row players should react by backing off the net, indicating they do not intend to attempt blocking the ball. This movement, reinforced by verbal information (e.g. "free ball", "free") should bring all players to adapt their position, assuming what we can call free ball formation. The players should be in their proper court position <u>before</u> the third contact by the opponents.

Whatever pattern a team uses to defend on a free ball, these principles should be observed:

- the setter must be out of the defence pattern and in position to set
- all players must be concerned with passing the ball to the setter before preparing to attack
- the formation should be adapted according to the location of the player sending the free ball.

Free ball With W Formation

Many teams will find advantageous to use this formation to defend on free ball, especially those using it for serve reception.

As seen in Figures 17 to 20, the movement of back row players will be determined by two factors:

- initial defensive system (e.g. 6-up or 6-back)
- position of the setter

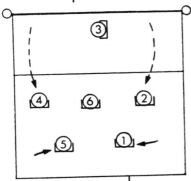

Figure 17:
Free ball with:
- 6-Up defence
- Setter in position #3

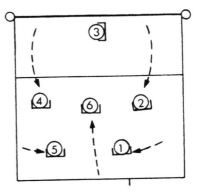

Figure 18
Free ball with:
- 6-back defence
- Setter in position #3

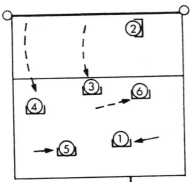

Figure 19
Free ball with:
- 6-up defence
- Setter in position #2

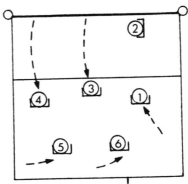

Figure 20
Free ball with:
- 6-back defence
- Setter in position #2

As mentioned, the players must move to their position before the third contact by the opponent. Although the W formation on free ball respects the same principles as for serve reception, the formation can vary as a free ball can come from different positions. The principle of equidistance of players at the top points of the pattern to the opponent sending the ball should be maintained (Figures 21 and 22).

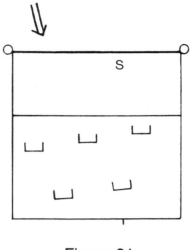

Figure 21

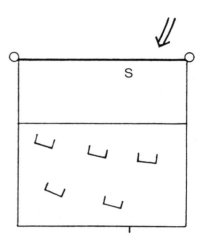

Figure 22

DRILLS

SERVE RECEPTION TO ATTACK

Drill 1

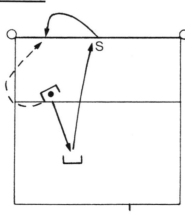

- groups of 3, one ball
- attacker tosses ball to passer, bumps to setter, setter sets outside
- attacker goes out of court then approaches, jumps and catches ball
- passer and setter cover
- 5x and switch
  a) medium or high sets
  b) other types of sets

Drill 2

- same as previous drill
- now attacker jumps and tips ball <u>back</u> at players covering
- one player digs other player sets high ball
- attacker goes out of court again, approaches and jumps and
  a) catches ball
  b) tips down the line
  c) spikes ball cross court

Drill 3

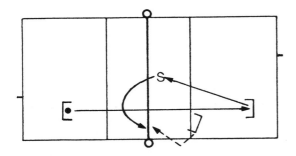

- groups of 4, one ball

- same as drill #1, but add server

  a) 1/2 court serve

  b) full court serve

  c) same as drill #2

  d) other types of sets

DEFENCE TO ATTACK

Drill 4

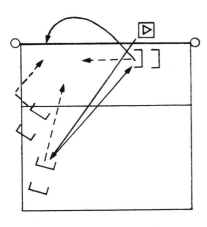

- Coach on chair spikes ball cross court at defenders
- Players dig balls, setter sets to attacker
- digger and setter cover
- 6 'good' ones and rotate
  a) attacker tips to target
  b) attacker spikes cross court
  c) attacker tips at players covering
  d) coach spikes at other digging positions
  e) other sets

Drill 5

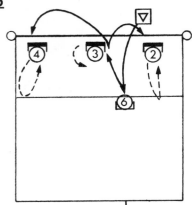

- 3 blockers and 1 tip digger
- coach tips ball over block to position 6
- attackers 4 and 2 get off net to prepare for attack
- setter 3 gets to ball and sets 'good' set
- 6 and 3 cover
- attacker:
   a) catches ball
   b) tips to target
   c) spikes to target
   d) tips back at players covering

FREE BALL TO ATTACK

Drill 6

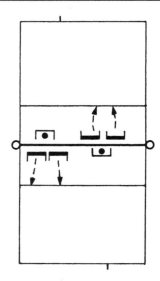

- groups of 3, one ball
- attacker with ball, tosses ball 2-3m in air and then volleys over the net to blockers
- on the toss, blockers call 'free' and shuffle off net to prepare, one player calls the ball and volleys the ball to the other player by the net
- set and passer approaches, setter covers
   a) catch ball
   b) tip ball over net
   c) tip ball back at cover, set partner

Drill 7

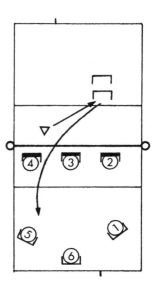

- coach tosses balls to players in line
- players volley or bump back over net
- on coach's toss, defence calls 'free' and moves into position to receive free ball
- volley to setter
- attackers
   a) catch ball
   b) tip to coach
   c) spike cross court
   d) tip back at players covering
   e) spike ball to target and coach tosses second ball over net at players covering

SUMMARY

- The cyclical nature of volleyball involves a continuous sequence of tasks for all players on the court

- All determined patterns used by a team should rely on:

  - the basic principles in respect to the task

  - the opponent's characteristics

- Proper use of a simple team system will bring better results than an uncontrolled advanced system

BASIC COACHING SKILLS

By Claude Lapré

BASIC COACHING SKILLS

The volleyball coach is often required to get actively involved in practice. These interventions are possible by control of certain skills referred to as the coaching skills. The quality of these skills will be a decisive factor in the improvement of your players.

By controlling directly the rhythm, specific load, speed and trajectory of the ball, the coach can place his/her athletes in favorable conditions. His/her ability to ball handle will influence the percentage of success of the athletes in the drill, a determining improvement factor. Ball handling will also permit an individualized and optimal work load for each athlete.

Upon completion of this unit, the coach will have a better understanding of:

- the criteria of efficient ball handling

- the basic ball handling skills

- how to organize a team in coach oriented drills

CRITERIA FOR EFFICIENCY

These criteria must be respected for an efficient, constructive intervention. Lack of ability to respect these will place the athletes in difficult, uncontrolled conditions unfavorable to skill improvement. Practice and good use of the acquired abilities are necessary.

ACCURACY

Accuracy means directing the ball at a precise/determined target. Lack of accuracy will bring the athlete to develop skill faults, hindering his/her performance in game situations.

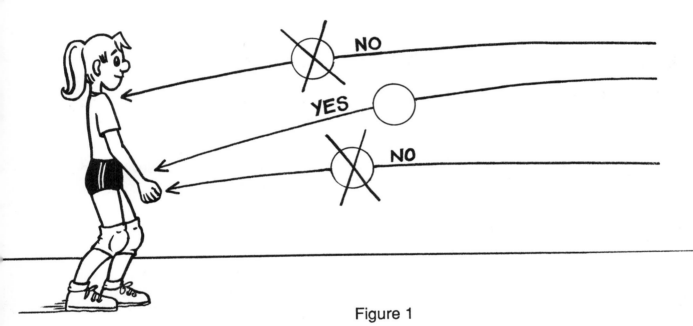

Figure 1

For beginners, when tossing and hitting, the ball should be directed in front of the player, that is between the player and the target. The trajectory should bring the ball between the waist and the knees. Speed is determined by the player's ability, but the ball must be _falling_ (Figure 1).

REGULARITY

A good ball handler is known for his/her regularity. He/she stands out by his/her ability to maintain during the drill:

- the same specific load

- the same rhythm

- the same accuracy

Lack of regularity offsets the athlete in his/her skill execution, breaks his/her concentration and may create hesitation and fear (Figure 2).

Figure 2

OBSERVATION AND INTERVENTION

A common problem in ball handling is the difficulty to observe the athletes and intervene. The coach often hits or tosses balls without consideration for correct skill execution.

Appropriate ball handling skills will make it possible for the coach to observe and correct, with timely interventions, maintaining rhythm and dosage.

SPATIAL ORIENTATION

While ball handling, the coach must respect spatial orientation characteristics of volleyball. This will be reflected by his/her placement on the court and logical trajectories, as shown in these examples for serve reception (Figure 3) and defence (Figure 4).

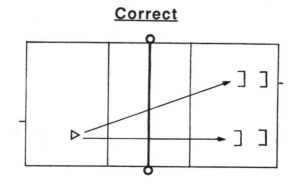

Correct

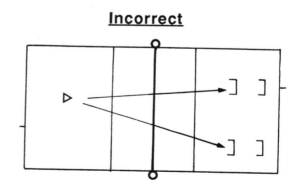

Incorrect

Figure 3

Correct	**Incorrect**

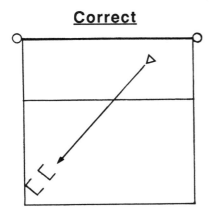

Figure 4

Another factor will be consideration of the opponent's preferred tactics or skills in serve and attack. This information will guide the coach in selecting the appropriate drills and influence his/her ball handling.

BASIC BALL HANDLING SKILLS

TOSSING

Tossing for Defence

Objective: Create stable and controlled conditions for improvement of basic skills in movement, positioning and free ball defence.

Skill Description: (Figure 5)

○ Front foot points towards the target

○ Ball held waist high

○ Wrist and forearm action; length and speed of movement according to distance of target.

○ Ball waist high

○ Hands on each side of the ball

○ Be careful for exaggerated, unrealistic ball spin

Figure 5

Drill Example:

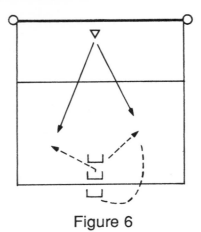

Figure 6

- Group of 3 players; 10 balls/player

- Coach (Δ) tosses the ball alternatively to the left and right

- Players move and catch or contact the ball (according to coach's instruction) with forearm or overhand pass

Tossing for Attack:

Objective: Create stable and controlled conditions for improvement of basic skills in attack.

Skill Description: (Figure 7)

o Foot close to the net is in front and pointing towards the target: The coach should be able to see the player from the start of his/her action to the moment of contact, without moving.

o Ball held waist high

o Same wrist and forearm action as when tossing for defence.

Trajectory for beginners should respect these guidelines:

o Tosses are not too close to net
o The trajectory brings the ball between the coach (re setter) and the player's initial position
o The ball should travel parallel or away from the net (towards the player)

Figure 7

Drill Example: (Figure 8)

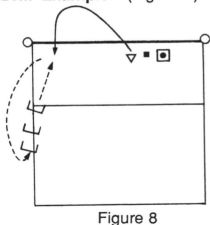

Figure 8

- Group of 3 players; 10 balls/player

- Coach (Δ) tosses high ball

- Players tip or hit the ball (according to coach's instruction)

HITTING

Hitting for Serve Reception:

Objective: Create stable and controlled conditions for improvement of basic skills in serve reception.

Skill Description of Sidearm Serve: (Figure 9)

- Coach stands sideways, shoulder opposite to hitting arm closer to the net
- Ball held waist high or slightly higher, with one hand
- Hitting action by forearm; added power can come from two sources: (1) hip action just before contact, and (2) holding hand bringing ball towards hitting hand for contact

The coach should look at the receiving player. A correct position and skill will enable him/her to serve with just a very quick look at the ball.

In his/her initial position, the coach must respect the relation with the service zone. However, he/she can change the distance from which he/she serves, to change rhythm and trajectory according to the ability of the players.

Figure 9

Drill Example: (Figure 10)

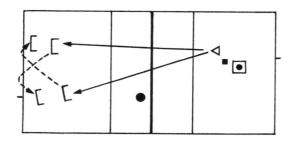

Figure 10

º Group of 4 players; 10 balls/player

º Coach (Δ) is at mid-court, in line with the serving zone; alternates serves in 5 and 1

º Players pass the ball to target; change of position after each pass

Hitting for Defence:

Objective: Create stable and controlled conditions for improvement of basic skills in backcourt defence.

Skill Description: (Figure 11)

º Opposite foot to hitting arm is forward and points towards target

º Ball raised by one hand, hit with the other hand with a short arm action

º Point of contact head high, slightly in front of body

º Added power can come from weight transfer and forward movement of upper body.

Proper skill will enable the coach to keep a constant view of the target/player, even at the moment of contact.

Players should take information from the coach's step orientation for direction and from his/her arm action for timing.

Figure 11

Drill Example: (Figure 12)

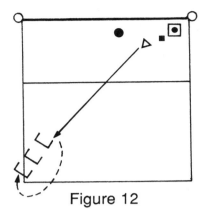

Figure 12

o Group of 3 players; 10 balls/player

o Coach hits ball in 5

o Players pass ball to target

Hitting for Blocking:

Objective: Create stable and controlled conditions for improvement of basic skills in blocking.

Skill Description:

o Position is similar to player hitting
o Ball is hit towards blocker's hand, with or without jumping (may stand on table or bench)
o Timing given to player by toss before hit

Drill Example: (Figure 13)

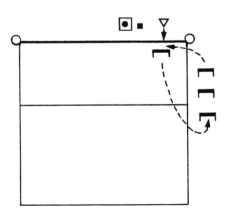

Figure 13

o Group of 4 players; 10 balls/player

o Coach hits ball in hands of player blocking in 2

o Player blocks ball

ORGANIZING COACH ORIENTED DRILLS

Quality ball handling by the coach is not sufficient to guarantee the success of coach oriented drills. The athletes must also get involved and perform their assigned task. By looking at the following diagram, we can identify these tasks (Figure 14).

- **Feeder (▪)**: Works in close collaboration with the coach; <u>gives</u> ball where the coach wants it (usually hip); should also count balls

- **Involved Players (⊔)**: Directly concerned by the drill; their movement should not bother partners or break drill rhythm

- **Shaggers (•)**: Shag balls or designed as target; they are responsible for the safety of the involved players

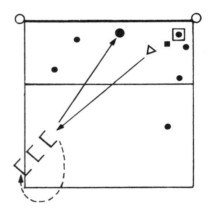

Figure 14

Aiming for efficiency in a drill should never be to the detriment of safety. Players involved must be worry free to concentrate on the objective of the drill.

Good ball handling will bring added possibilities to a coach, in controlling variables influencing the development of his/her players. Of course, improvement will request practice. But every coach owes it to his/her athletes.

SUMMARY

- Efficient ball handling will respect these criteria:

    o Accuracy
    o Regularity
    o Observation and intervention
    o Spatial orientation

- Ball handling skills which can be used are:

    o Tossing: For defence
                 For attack

    o Hitting: For serve reception
                 For backcourt defence
                 For blocking

- Coach oriented drills require an efficient team organization. Players can be: Feeding
                 Shagging or target
                 Involved in the drill

- Shaggers are also responsible for safety.

- Ball handling offers many possibilities to the coach. But practice is the only road to improvement.

INJURY PREVENTION

By Guntis Obrascovs

INJURY PREVENTION

The game of volleyball is a dynamic and explosive activity. It is important to understand the nature of the game itself in order to formulate the ideas and policies necessary to minimize the risk of injury during participation. After completion of this unit, the coach will have a better understanding of:

- injury prevention

- factors affecting warm-up and cool-down

- factors affecting flexibility

INJURY PREVENTION

There is no doubt that injuries of some sort or another will occur during volleyball activities. Some of these injuries are unavoidable. They are natural occurrences during activity.

However, we rarely maximize the precautions and events that should be followed, in order to eliminate those injuries which might have been prevented with a little more common sense or a little more attention.

This second type of injury can be illustrated by looking at this situation (Figure 1).

"Hit this ball in 5, Paul."

"Good. Now this ball in 1. . .Paul?"

This type of incident usually results in a minor sprain of the player's ankle. It is important to realize that this scene could have been avoided if there existed and was enforced, a policy of picking up all loose balls immediately. Most teams have this type of procedure but sometimes are lazy in their execution.

The game of volleyball is played on a court that has defined and visible boundaries. However, the events during a game or practice see a lot of action that takes place outside of the lines of the court. This is an environmental consideration that is not present in a lot of other team sports where play outside of the court is rare.

Any injury prevention program must start with a daily check of the playing surface and playing area. The best idea would be a checklist that is followed everyday by players and gymnasium staff.

INJURY PREVENTION CHECKLIST

Item	Problem	Correction
Net area and posts	Loose attenae	Should be tied
	Hole in net	Should be repaired, at least temporarily
	Exposed wires	Taped down and ends taped
	Exposed area on stand or posts	Should be padded
Playing surface	Dusty floor	Should be cleaned
	Wet floor	Should be dried
	Missing plugs	Find and put in place or temporarily cover hole
	Loose boards on wooden floor	Should be secured
Surrounding area	Other apparatus and equipment such as mobile equipment	Should be removed and stored properly
	Fixed sharp objects or non-yielding surfaces	Should be padded
Other	Check for any hazardous equipment such as: - loose ceiling tiles - dangerous lighting system - chairs, benches - bleachers misplaced	Act accordingly You may also have to modify your planned practice.

PRACTICE PROCEDURES

The next important aspect of injury prevention is that the procedures during practice minimize the chance of injury. The most important consideration here is that of loose balls on the floor.

A lot of volleyball training uses continuous drills of a repetitive nature. In running an offence, the coach may have ten balls hit in a time span of thirty seconds. This means that on the tenth ball, there are nine other balls that may wind up under the net or under the players jumping during play. The coach that has his team well drilled in shagging and picking up loose balls will not have to worry about this possiblity.

If players are instructed and drilled in the habit of picking up balls immediately, many potential injury situations will be avoided.

Two other areas that the coach has an influence on during practise with respect to injury prevention are i) proper technique execution, and ii) equipment (non-ball) placement.

The athlete that exhibits the proper jumping and landing techniques will not be involved with potentially dangerous situations with respect to net play. The principle mechanism that I am thinking about here, is that of a blocker and spiker jumping across the net from each other (Figure 2). The blocker lands before the spiker, with his feet on the offensive side of the net, and the spiker lands on the foot of the blocker. The net result is a potentially significant sprained ankle.

Equipment such as ball carts should be placed on the court so that it does not interfere with the normal function of the athlete. Equipment should not be placed in "blind spots" with respect to each athlete's playing area.

WARM-UP TO COOL-DOWN

The human body is a very formidable machine. It is capable of tremendous physical accomplishments. It cannot work at maximum efficiency without warming up a little beforehand. It also will recover much more quickly and more efficiently post-activity with a proper cool down period. These two aspects of athletic activity are the two most neglected and least understood by the individual athlete.

WARM-UP

The warm-up period is crucial to gaining the most out of each athletic session. It is a period of time that is often cut short so that "we can get on with the practice". It is important from both a physical and mental point of view that the athlete is introduced slowly into a high intensity athletic endeavour.

The principle aim of a proper warm-up is to:

- elevate the body temperature to a working level.
- rehearse the events that will go on during the activity.
- put the athlete into a 'volleyball' mental state of mind.

The physiological results of a proper warm-up are:

- increase the efficiency of oxygen delivery to the working areas.
- reduce muscle viscosity in order to improve mechanical efficiency.
- possible reduction of injuries during activity.
- nervous impulse travel more rapidly and the sensitivity of nerve receptors is augmented.
- nerve impulses are geared for the execution of the complex, coordinated movements of body parts needed in the game of volleyball.
- the muscles will experience an increase in blood flow and therefore an increase in body temperature. This will allow for a more efficient delivery of nutrients to the exercising muscle and aid in an efficient removal of the resulting waste products.

The warm-up period includes many different aspects for consideration. The athlete will need to get actively moving by an activity such as running or skipping rope. The athlete will need to rehearse the basic skills needed in volleyball, e.g. volleying, bumping, spiking, etc. The team will have to work on some type of team play to set the stage for playing. The amount of time that a coach will spend on each of these areas depends on the types of athletes that he has, what level of play they are at, the goal of the practice or game, etc.

One aspect of the warm-up that is often cut short is the flexibility section. This is the section that deals with the conscious performance of certain exercises for the objective of stretching specific muscle groups that will be used during the activity. The flexibility portion does not include calisthenics, toe-touching, etc. It is a period of time, minimum of ten minutes, that is used to prepare the body for activity.

GENERAL CONSIDERATIONS OF A FLEXIBILITY ROUTINE

There are basically two types of stretching techniques that are available for the individual who is stretching. One is the "ballistic" technique which uses bouncing or jerky movements to increase flexibility. The other method is called the "static" technique which uses slow stretches and "hold" positions to increase flexibility.

Research has shown that both methods have worked in terms of increasing flexibility. However, the "ballistic" technique can cause injuries to the structures being stretched because of the "bouncy" nature of its performance. Therefore, the "static" method of stretching is preferred because it is less threatening in its execution.

In understanding the fundamental differences between the two techniques, it is important to consider a physiological response called the <u>stretch reflex</u>. One component of the stretch reflex is found in the muscle spindle. When the muscle is stretched, a signal is sent to contract the muscle to prevent overextension. The force of this contraction is proportional to the force of the stretch.

If we look at this response, we can see that in the improper execution of a "ballistic" style stretch, we could have a situation where we are actively elongating a muscle, and at the same time have that same muscle contracting proportionally to the amount of stretch being induced. This simultaneous stretching and contracting could result in a minor injury to the muscle itself. It is for this reason that the "static" form of stretching is recommended.

There are many forms of "static" stretching with respect to the length of time to hold the muscle and the number of repetitions. We have found the following sequence to be an effective form that is quite time efficient.

We take the muscle being stretched and perform the exercise until the point where you "feel" the stretch. It should not be a painful feeling. At this point we "hold" the stretch for a count of eight, while we try to relax the muscle being stretched and to relax the surrounding structure. After "eight" we should be able to increase the stretch a little further, until we "feel" the stretch again. We hold this position for another count of eight and then return to the starting position. Usually one or two performances of each exercise is sufficient.

This method allows for easy identification of the muscle being stretched by the individual and also allows the individual to experience the feeling of the muscle elongating with the development of the stretch. This use and control of "relaxation" is an invaluable physical and mental tool for the athlete.

Before undertaking a flexibility program, an athlete should recognize that his/her flexibility is, foremost, an individual consideration and, secondly, variant from day to day or time to time. Comparisons should be made with the athlete himself not with others around the athlete.

Factors affecting flexibility include:

- warm-up
- keeping body parts warm during performance
- age
- sex (females are usually more flexible)
- specificity to each particular joint

IMPORTANT ASPECTS OF A STRETCHING PROGRAM

Any stretching program should be preceded by a short bout of activity, e.g. easy running or skipping, in order to elevate the body temperature.

The program selected should be geared to the needs of the sport itself and to the athlete's individual needs. Any good volleyball stretching program will consider the fact that the game requires the use of both upper and lower bodies and therefore, equal time should be spent on both areas. Another important consideration in any program is that opposite groups of muscles should both be worked on - this means both biceps and triceps should be worked on and both the hamstrings and the quadriceps need attention. One can set a "tunnel vision" with respect to the whole body's need for stretching.

The "static" technique should be used with each specific exercise. It is imperative that the athlete knows which muscle group is being stretched by each exercise. This knowledge will allow him to use his concentration and relaxation skills to optimally perform each exercise. A lot of time can be wasted by the aimless execution of stretching type actions without using any body feedback.

Flexibility is a simple effective tool for the athlete to better prepare for activity. If performed with the patience, proper technique and concentration necessary, any athlete can improve his individual flexibility.

One other technique for stretching that is available is called the P.N.F. (Proprioceptive Neuromuscular Facilitation) technique. It is a partner stretching technique that uses the physiological response that after a maximum muscular contraction you get a maximum relaxation of that muscle. It is a very effective method. Its drawbacks are that i) because two people are needed for each exercise, the stretching time period is being doubled, and ii) the fact that two people are working in conjunction with each other, poor communication can lead to improper execution and maybe a slight injury.

In viewing the technique, we can see why some people call it the "hold and relax" technique. Athlete "A" is being stretched and athlete "B" is helping in the stretch. The muscle being considered is stretched by "B" to a point where "A" feels the stretch. "A" then contracts the muscle being stretched as hard as he can for a count of six (this figure varies from program to program). The muscle being contracted is slowly contracted and relaxed so that there is no sudden, violent force applied to the muscle.

After the six count, "A" relaxes the muscle and "B" helps to stretch the muscle further into the range until a new stretch is felt. This "stretch-contract" sequence is repeated for a total of three executions and the exercise is terminated by a final stretch. One, therefore, commences and finishes with a stretch. The partners reverse positions and perform the same sequence.

It is important that all commands are done verbally. One should hear the words "stop" - "contract" - one...two...three...four contraction. Both partners have to know exactly what is going on.

COOL-DOWN

The "cool-down" portion of an activity sees the gradual dropback of the body from an active to a rest level. The proper use of such a period post activity can go a long way towards reducing post exercise stiffness and tightness.

The body, generally, likes the gradual change from one state to another. It does not react well to sudden changes in intensity and activity. If we roughly graphed the ideal volleyball session, the body would much prefer Figure 3 than Figure 4.

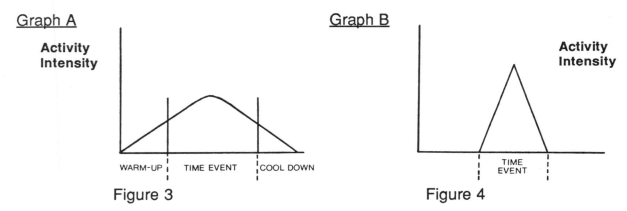

Graph A

Graph B

Figure 3

Figure 4

The cool-down will allow the body to reduce some of the waste products produced during activity from the areas of exercise and also will allow the individual to stretch out muscles that are tight from activity.

One should include a relaxed run of about five minutes and performing his stretching routine again, during the "cool-down" period. One can also include lying on one's back with the legs elevated and "shaking" or "bicycling" the legs. The entire period is generally less structured than the warm-up period.

In general,the proper use of "warm-up" and "cool-down" periods will go a long way to keeping the athlete healthy and feeling well while experiencing the particular demands of the game of volleyball.

SUMMARY

- Precautions should be maximized to prevent injuries.

- An "Injury Prevention Checklist" could be used to prevent most dangerous situations.

- Proper skill execution will prevent injuries.

- Proper warm-up will enable the athlete to perform with maximum efficiency.

- Static stretching is effective and safe.

- Flexibility can be improved. In doing so, the athlete should work on upper and lower bodies and opposite groups of muscles.

- Cool-down will reduce post exercise stiffness and favour quick recovery.

BASIC RULES
AND REGULATIONS

By Claude Lapré

BASIC RULES
AND REGULATIONS

It is the responsibility of all participants in a sport to know and abide by the rules of the game. And, unless you want your athletes to get involved in a referee clinic, you will be their source of reference for learning the rules.

A knowledge of what is going on is necessary for the athletes to feel comfortable in a competitive situation. Therefore, you will have to instruct your athletes on the basic rules and regulations. If not, they will often be distracted by situations they do not understand, which will hinder their performance, deteriorate the value of training and limit the rewards they should derive from efforts in practice.

Let us go through a quick test covering volleyball's basic rules, after which a few "coaching tips" can be discussed.

Upon completion of this unit, the coach will have a better understanding of:

- What are the basic rules of volleyball

- How to introduce the basic rules to the players

- How to act in basic game coaching situations

EVALUATE YOUR KNOWLEDGE OF THE RULES

QUESTION 1

The court dimensions are: (Rule 1.1.1.)

a) 30 feet x 60 feet
b) 10 metres x 20 metres
c) 9 metres x 18 metres

QUESTION 2

The front zone is limited by the attack line placed: (Rule 1.5.1.)

a) 3 metres from the middle of the centre line, and by both side lines
b) 4 metres from the middle of the center line, and by both side lines
c) 3 metres from the middle of the center line and considered to be extended indefinitely

QUESTION 3

The height of the net shall be: (Rule 2.4.1. and 2.4.2.)

a) 2.35 metres for men and 2.15 metres for women, measured at the ends
b) 2.43 metres for men and 2.24 metres for women, measured at the ends
c) 2.35 metres for men and 2.15 metres for women, measured at the centre
d) 2.43 metres for men and 2.24 metres for women, measured at the centre

QUESTION 4

A team shall consist of a maximum of: (Rule 4.1.1.)

a) 6 players
b) 10 players
c) 12 players
d) 15 players

QUESTION 5

During a game, I can ask the referee an explanation or interpretation of the rules. Who am I? (Rule 5.5.3. and 5.5.5.)

a) The coach
b) A player on the court
c) A player out of the court
d) The team captain
e) The game captain

QUESTION 6

This is not a question. But let's take a break and read Rule #6 from the CVA Rule Book.

Rule 6.   Coaches

6.1.   RESPONSIBILITIES OF THE COACH
The coach is responsible for the conduct and discipline of the players.

6.1.1.   Prior to the game, he/she must register, check the names and numbers of his/her players on the score sheet and place his/her signature on it.

6.1.2.   Prior to each set (game) he/she must give the scorer or the second referee the line-up sheet duly completed and signed.

6.1.3.   He/she may direct warm-up sessions of his/her players on the playing court prior to the match.

6.1.4.   During the match he/she must sit down on the players bench, in close proximity to the scorer, and must be the nearest person, on the bench, to the scorer.

6.1.5.   Only during time-outs and intervals between sets may the coach give instructions. These instructions must be given without entering the court or delaying the game.

6.2.   RESPONSIBILITIES OF THE
ASSISTANT COACH

6.2.1.   He/she sits on the players' bench, but has no rights.

6.2.2.   In the event the coach must leave his/her team, the assistant coach may assume his/her responsibilities with the authorization of the first referee, at the request of the team captain.

6.3.   COACHES' CONDUCT

6.3.1.   They are obliged to respect and make their players respect the referees, spectators, organizers and opponents.

6.3.2.   They cannot dispute, argue, or request clarifications of the referees on their decisions.

QUESTION 7

Before a match, the first referee carries out a toss up in the presence of the two team captains. The winner: (Rule 7.1.1.)

a) gets the right to serve and choice of court
b) gets the right to serve
c) gets the choice of court
d) chooses the court or the right to serve

QUESTIONS 8 TO 10 (Figures 1 to 3)

Indicate, in the following diagrams, if the team is in proper position at the moment of the opponent's serve: (Rule 9.)

8. 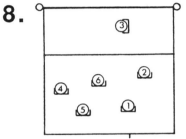   **9.** 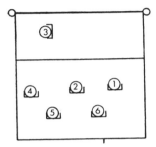   **10.**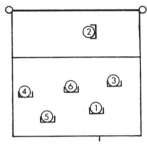

Figure 1   Figure 2   Figure 3
Correct ☐   Correct ☐   Correct ☐
Incorrect ☐   Incorrect ☐   Incorrect ☐

QUESTION 11

How many time-outs and substitutions are allowed per team per set?

(Rule 10.2.)

a) Three (3) time-outs and six (6) substitutions
b) Two (2) time-outs and six (6) substitutions
c) Three (3) time-outs and three (3) substitutions
d) Two (2) time-outs and three (3) substitutions

QUESTION 12

Which sequence(s) of substitutions is (are) legal, for the same team in the same game?   (Rules 11.1.1. and 11.2.3.)

a) Player #1 for #3; 3 for 6; 12 for 5; 7 for 4; 11 for 2; 5 for 12
b) Player #2 for #10; 6 for 8; 1 for 4; 8 for 6; 13 for 7
c) Player #1 for #12; 6 for 9; 8 for 2; 12 for 1; 13 for 4; 9 for 6; 2 for 8
d) Player #3 for #7; 12 for 9; 7 for 3; 5 for 6; 8 for 7

QUESTION 13

The ball may be contacted...   (Rule 15.3.)

a)   with any part of the body
b)   with the arms, forearms and hands
c)   with any part of the body above and including the waist
d)   with the arms, forearms, hands and head

QUESTION 14 (Figure 4)

Identify which ball(s) is (are) crossing the net correctly.   (Rule 16.)

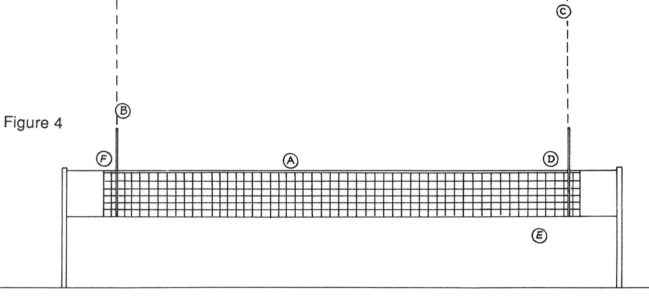

Figure 4

QUESTION 15 (Figure 5)

Identify the situation(s) where there is an illegal contact with the opponent's court. (Rule 17.4.)

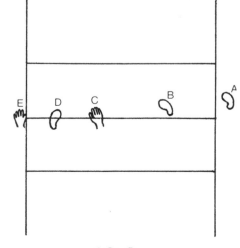

QUESTIONS 16 TO 30

Match the following hand signals with the correct meaning.

16. _____

17. _____

18. _____

19. _____

20. _____

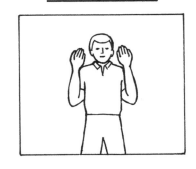

21. _____

22. _____

23. _____

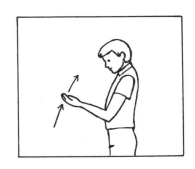

24. _____

25. _____

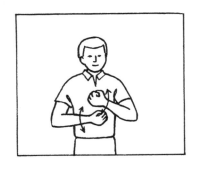

26. _____

27. _____

28. _____   **29.** _____   **30.** _____

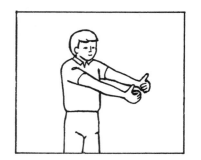   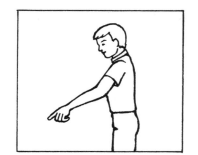   

Meaning:

a) Point
b) Change courts
c) End of game
d) Service - foot fault
e) Position/Rotation fault

f) Ball out
g) Double contact
h) Four hits
i) Held ball
j) Touched ball

k) Contact below waist
l) Centre line fault
m) Double fault
n) Time-out
o) Substitution

ANSWERS AT END OF THIS UNIT

INTRODUCING BASIC RULES
TO YOUR PLAYERS

When introducing knowledge of the rules to our players, we should remember their sources of motivation. Usually, they play volleyball for pleasure, with consideration to the benefits of the physical activity and of the social aspects. Any knowledge we introduce should be geared at increasing these benefits.

Rules will be explained as it becomes necessary. Why explain back-line hitting possibilities and restrictions if we play in a calibre where serve and serve reception is 90% of the game? Essential basic rules are limited at early stages: number of players on the court, service rotation, how to score a point, how to win a set, number of contacts, net and line faults.

Players should be concerned with rules only in a perspective of guiding their athletic efforts and performance in the proper direction. Once they acquire sufficient knowledge to understand most situations that can come up, they should concentrate on how they can influence the outcome: play harder, play better.

BASIC GAME
COACHING SITUATIONS

Coaches often seem to be more concerned with gaining minimal (and questionable) advantages by stretching the rules than by proper use of the same rules. Volleyball limits the possibilities of intervention by the coach, during a match: limited substitutions in number and in form, limited time-outs in number and in time, limited time between sets and no interventions from the bench during a game. While it is often possible to "stretch" these rules, it may be to our team's disadvantage.

All these rules are geared at creating a situation of autonomy and self reliance for the players on the court, increasing the mental and emotional requirements of the game. Trying to limit these effects may help your team on a short term but can also limit it's long term potential.

Major problems can also be created in trying to gain a minimal advantage. Waiting to the last second to ask a time-out or a substitution may seem a good idea, until it is refused for being too late. Preventing problems is more useful. For example, two minutes between sets is a short time but can be used properly if you prepare line-ups and comments in advance.

Being aware and using the possibilities offered by the rules will be more productive than looking for loopholes.

QUIZ ANSWERS

Count one (1) point for each correct answer (Maximum score: 29)

Question	1.	c	11.	b	21.	g
	2.	c	12.	b	22.	l
	3.	d	13.	c	23.	i
	4.	c	14.	a,b,d	24.	k
	5.	e	15.	b,c	25.	o
	6.	-	16.	a	26	h
	7.	d	17.	e	27.	n
	8.	Correct	18.	c	28.	m
	9.	Incorrect	19.	b	29.	d
	10.	Incorrect	20.	f	30.	j

<u>Rating:</u> **If your score is**

from 26 to 29: Your knowledge of basic rules is excellent
from 20 to 25: Your knowledge of basic rules is acceptable, but should be improved
from 0 - 20:   You must improve your knowledge of basic rules

SUMMARY

- Every player should have a basic knowledge of the rules and regulations.

- It is the coach's responsibility to introduce the rules to his/her players.

- Introduction of rules is done during practice, in relation to the situations involved in drills.

- The coach should plan the use of time-outs and substitutions before a match.

- 'Heads up' coaching will give better results than trying to stretch the rules.

VOLLEYBALL ADMINISTRATIVE STRUCTURES

By: Claude Lapré
Lorne Sawula

VOLLEYBALL ADMINISTRATIVE STRUCTURES

Many coaches go through years of involvement with limited knowledge of their Local, Regional and National Associations. Then, one day, out of necessity for a specific service, they establish a first contact. For some, it is a revealing experience.

These associations exist for your service. You owe it to yourself and to your players to establish contact and participate in their activities.

Upon completion of this unit, the coach will have a better understanding of:

- the origins of volleyball

- the International Volleyball Federation Structure

- the Canadian Volleyball Association history, structure and services

- the Regional Volleyball Associations structure and services

Information concerning the FIVB from: Olympic Encyclopedia, September 1985; International Olympic Committee, 1985; pp. 5-19.

HISTORY OF THE FIVB

1895 - THE INVENTION OF VOLLEYBALL

An American, William G. Morgan (1870-1942), born in the State of New York, has gone down in history as the inventor of the game of Volleyball, to which he first gave the name "Mintonette".

While a student at the YMCA College at Springfield, W.G. Morgan met James Naismith, who in 1891 had invented basketball. Morgan discovered the sport, and took it up.

In 1894, he was appointed Director of Physical Education at the YMCA section at Holyoke, in Massachussets. He noticed that basketball did not suit all his students, particularly the businessmen who came in the evening. He became aware of the need for a more recreational game which, while not involving any contact, would call for intense effort and thus ensure complete relaxation without any risk of injury. In an article published in 1915, he explained,

"I did not know of any sport like volleyball to help me, what we thought up was the fruit of experience acquired in a gymnasium..."

In his view, tennis provided a good many advantages but required racquets, balls, a net and various equipment rather impractical for working in a group. First of all, he retained the idea of using the net. He placed it at about 6 feet 6 inches above the ground (1 m. 98), just above the height of an average man. He tried out various balls. The basketball was too heavy and too big; he took out the inner tube, but the ball was then too light.

Finally, he had a leather ball made by the firm A.G. Spalding & Bros., with a rubber inner tube; he was satisfied with the result. We are now in 1895.

A meeting of YMCA Physical Education directors was organized at Springfield. Morgan was invited to demonstrate his game. Two teams each made up of five members went with him. One was led by J.J. Curran and the other by John Lynch, who were respectively Mayor and Fire Chief of Holyoke. Morgan stated, *"The exhibition took place in the gymnasium of the College to the satisfaction of all, I think."*

Professor Alfred T. Halstead, who was present at this demonstration, suggested that the name "Mintonette" be replaced by "Volleyball" which was more suggestive and descriptive of the action.

The rules were first printed in 1897 in the handbook of the North American YMCA Athletic League.

ITS EXPANSION THROUGHOUT THE WORLD

Thanks to those in charge at the YMCA, volleyball quickly became popular in all United States territories and Canada. Elwood S. Brown introduced it to the Philippines by raising the number of players to sixteen to enable a greater participation in matches.

In 1908, Heinzo Omori, having completed his studies at Springfield, and Frank H. Brown, Physical Education Director at the YMCA in Tokyo brought it to Japan. J. Oward Crocker promoted it in China and J.H. Gray in Burma and India. In 1913, volleyball appeared on the programme of the Far-Eastern Games, organized at Manila according to the "Brown" rules. The team from the Philippines won.

From then on, the development of this sport on the Asian continent was assured, although for a long time the rules remained different to the American rules.

In 1916, the YMCA managed to induce the powerful National Collegiate Athletic Association (NCAA) to publish its rules and a series of articles contributing to the rapid growth of volleyball amongst young college students.

In 1918 the number of players per team was limited to six and in 1922 the maximum number of authorized contacts with the ball was fixed at three.

Between 1917 and 1930, the Europeans discovered volleyball through an American expeditionary force and the YMCA centres. A volleyball section was set up in Czechoslovakia in 1920.

Three years later, the Czechoslovakian Basketball and Volleyball Federation became the first of its type. In 1922, the Bulgarians in turn took up volleyball, and later the Soviets followed suit.

In Spain, the Toledo Central School of Gymnastics published the first book of rules. The Japanese Federation was set up in 1927, a year before the American Volleyball Federation (USVBA). Since then the latter has published an annual guide.

In 1929, the Cubans organized the first tournament according to American rules as part of the Regional Games[1] recognized by the IOC. The team from Mexico won the gold medal. In 1933, El Savador organized the Central-American and Caribbean Games and added a women's tournament to the programme, played according to the American rules. Again, the Mexican team won.

THE BIRTH OF AN INTERNATIONAL FEDERATION

Shortly before the Second World War, international links were established in Europe, notably between Polish and French teams under Félix Castellant, first President of the French Federation, which had been set up in 1936.

In 1945, Harold T. Friermood (USA), then a member of the YMCA, and who rapidly became a leader in international volleyball[2], strove to establish international relations. He travelled, published and distributed many writings.

In Europe, in January 1946, the A.C. Sporta Prague team, at the time one of the best clubs in Czechoslovakia, travelled to Poland with a basketball team. During their stay in Warsaw, the Polish Volleyball Federation and its President, Mr. Wirszyllo, organized a match between its representatives and a few Czech members guided by Mr. Jerabek. One of those present, Vladimir Spirit, recalls, *"I was lucky enough to take part. The little meeting took place in the only undamaged part of the YMCA building; the capital of Poland had been completely destroyed by bombardments during the war. The electricity had been cut off and as a result we worked by the light of a kerosene lamp. The negotiations concerned the possible widening of contacts with some countries interested in volleyball as well as some tasks necessary for the foundation of the FIVB.*

The efforts of the two Federations (Czechoslovakia and Poland) were fruitful and our organization (The Czechoslovak Volleyball Federation, of which I was Secretary General, although still a university student) was successful in establishing useful relationships."

On the American continent, a South American Volleyball Confederation was founded on 12th February 1946 while on 12th May of the same year, Harold T. Friermood, who had become Secretary/Treasurer of the USVBA organized volleyball's Golden Jubilee at Chicago (1895-1896 to 1945-1946). He invited Avery Brundage, the future President of the International Olympic Committee, but who was then only Vice-President of the highest Olympic authority and President of the United States Olympic Committee.

The steps to be taken to achieve Olympic recognition were explained and Mr. Brundage prompted his fellow-countrymen to encourage the setting up of an International Federation. Friermood set sail for Europe, where he attended the Olympic Games at London.

On 27th August 1946, at Prague, the Czechoslovak team met the French team in the presence of 5,000 spectators. The Czechs won easily by 3 sets to 0. On the eve of the match, the French, Polish and Czech leaders met in the Smicho Café. Amongst them was Paul Libaud, the new President of the French Federation, together with his fellow countrymen Henri Aujard and Babin, Mr. Wirszyllo, President of the Polish Federation and his colleague Szeremeta, Mr. Havel, President of the Czech Federation, accompanied by Vladimir Spirit, Stolz, Cabalka, Krotsky and Pulkrab. Belgians, Romanians and Yugoslavs were involved by writing in the work. The basis of the FIVB was thus built and a meeting was fixed for the constituent congress planned in 1947; its organization was entrusted to Paul Libaud.

The French Federation set up this event and assisted in the formation of national federations in Belgium, Luxembourg, Holland and Switzerland. Also delegates from thirteen federations met in Paris as planned on 20th April 1947 to set up the International Volleyball Federation.

[1] Central American and Caribbean Games
[2] He presided over the USVBA, became Vice-President of the FIVB, and was an historian of renown.

Successive Presidents:

1947 - 1984:	Paul Libaud (FRA)
Since 1984:	Rubén Acosta (MEX)

Successive Secretaries General:

1947 - 1959:	Julien Lenoir (FRA)
1959 - 1978:	Henry Aujard (FRA)
1978 - 1982:	Anguel Barzachki (BUL)
Since 1982:	Chadly Zouiten (TUN)

Since then, through subsequent congresses, the FIVB structure has evolved to become one of the largest sport federations.

Major events to be noted include:

September 1949, Prague (TCH) - First Men's World Championship
August 1952, Moscow (URS) - First Women's World Championship
March 1955, Mexico (MEX) - Volleyball appeared on the program of the IInd Panamerican Games in Mexico
November 1955, Florence (ITA) - The Japanese Federation adopts the international rules and decides to gradually introduce them into Asia.
October 1964, Tokyo (JPN) - First Olympic titles are awarded to Japan (Women's) and USSR (Men's)
June 1966 - Recognition of a 5th Confederation for Central American and the Caribbean, under the presidency of Mr. Rubén Acosta (MEX)
October 1968, Mexico (MEX) - Canada and USA join the Central American and Caribbean zone, which thereafter becomes known as NORCECA.
September 1977 - First Junior Men's and Women's World Championship

Also, rules have been modified gradually and are constantly subject to discussion on specific items. These changes are only possible every four (4) years, on Olympic year. Although adjustments in interpretation sometimes leads to "local" changes during this period.

The following Organizational Chart (1985) will give you a general view of the FIVB structure (Chart 1).

Chart 1:   THE FIVB ADMINISTRATION

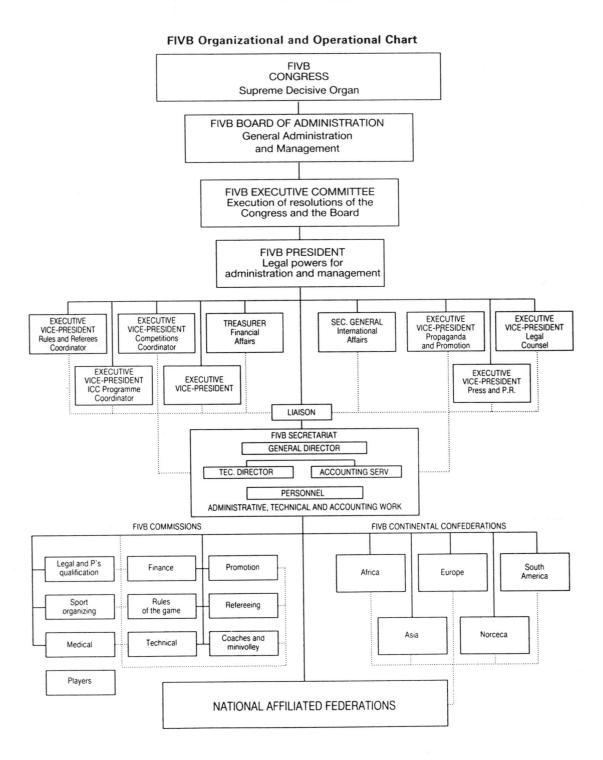

FIVB Organizational and Operational Chart

```
┌─────────────────────────────────────┐
│              FIVB                    │
│            CONGRESS                  │
│      Supreme Decisive Organ          │
└─────────────────────────────────────┘

┌─────────────────────────────────────┐
│   FIVB BOARD OF ADMINISTRATION       │
│       General Administration         │
│          and Management              │
└─────────────────────────────────────┘

┌─────────────────────────────────────┐
│     FIVB EXECUTIVE COMMITTEE         │
│    Execution of resolutions of the   │
│       Congress and the Board         │
└─────────────────────────────────────┘

┌─────────────────────────────────────┐
│          FIVB PRESIDENT              │
│         Legal powers for             │
│   administration and management      │
└─────────────────────────────────────┘
```

EXECUTIVE VICE-PRESIDENT Rules and Referees Coordinator

EXECUTIVE VICE-PRESIDENT Competitions Coordinator

TREASURER Financial Affairs

SEC. GENERAL International Affairs

EXECUTIVE VICE-PRESIDENT Propaganda and Promotion

EXECUTIVE VICE-PRESIDENT Legal Counsel

EXECUTIVE VICE-PRESIDENT ICC Programme Coordinator

EXECUTIVE VICE-PRESIDENT

EXECUTIVE VICE-PRESIDENT Press and P.R.

LIAISON

FIVB SECRETARIAT

GENERAL DIRECTOR

TEC. DIRECTOR

ACCOUNTING SERV

PERSONNEL

ADMINISTRATIVE, TECHNICAL AND ACCOUNTING WORK

FIVB COMMISSIONS

FIVB CONTINENTAL CONFEDERATIONS

Legal and P's qualification	Finance	Promotion
Sport organizing	Rules of the game	Refereeing
Medical	Technical	Coaches and minivolley
Players		

Africa — Europe — South America

Asia — Norceca

NATIONAL AFFILIATED FEDERATIONS

VOLLEYBALL IN CANADA

After the innovation of volleyball in the United States it soon spread to Canada (1900). The Ottawa Y.M.C.A. may have been the first place that volleyball was played in Canada. In later years other Y.M.C.A.'s included volleyball in their programs. As early as 1913, the first league was organized and one of the teams was the Toronto Central Y. Following the First World War a number of tournaments were set up. In 1920, the First Annual Y.M.C.A. Volleyball Championship for business men was held in Hamilton. The Ontario Volleyball Association was organized in 1928, as well as an association from the Prairie Provinces. Volleyball was mainly a Y.M.C.A. sport and restricted to being played in the Y.M.C.A.'s in Canada. Although there were various other organizations, such as the Manitoba Teacher's College, who played outside of the Y.M.C.A.

In the west inter-provincial play developed into the Western Canadian Championships and in the east the Eastern Canadian Championships developed into the Canadian Open National Finals. As early as 1938, the Kitchener-Waterloo Y.M.C.A. team travelled to Montreal to play their champions from the Y.M.C.A. The Ontario team won and were unofficially proclaimed the Eastern Canadian Champions. Any further development was stopped by the Second World War and it was not until 1947 that any inter-provincial meets were held. From this it led to, in 1948, a tournament which involved the Ottawa Y.M.C.A., the Montreal Y.M.C.A., Sherbrooke, and the Montreal Y.M.H.A. The latter finally won the tournament.

During and after the Second World War the exposure to military personnel served to change the game of volleyball into a strenuous major sport. Immigrants from European countries, where volleyball had eagerly spread, brought in their competitive spirit. They dominated the game in Canada and played it with such skill that it brought in a new attitude towards competition in the sport.

The first Canadian Championship was held in 1953. It was the first huge test of the Canadian Volleyball Association which was formed earlier in the year. Instead of having one body in one location dictating the sport it soon evolved into provincial regional associations who appointed their representatives to the national body.

International competition was started in 1959, as Canada entered a volleyball team in the Pan American Games. Government grants became available to assist groups in travelling and the situation changed fast in a short period. At frist the C.V.A. was financially unable to provide even uniforms for the Pan-American team. By 1967, a special fund raising committee was able to raise over $3,100.00 to support the men's and women's volleyball teams in the 1967 Pan American Games.

The government's first grant of $1,500.00 in 1962, helped the C.V.A. on its way. This was followed by $7,568.00 in 1963-64, $8,640.00 in 1964-65. The C.V.A. also took its own initiative and held many clinics and brought in other teams of high calibre to raise interest in the sport. The biggest project was a cross-country tour by the men's and women's teams of the U.S.S.R. and U.S.A. (1966).

In a five year period up to 1966, the C.V.A. benefitted by a total of $60,443.56 in government grants. Since then, C.V.A.'s competitive and administrative structure has matured to offer widespread services to its members.

For the competitive structure, the following events should be noted:

1965: First Canadian Junior Championship
1977: First Canadian Juvenile Championship
1980: First East and West Midget Championships
1981: First East and West Senior A Championships

Also, the educational structures have turned to volleyball as highlighted by the first Canadian Championships for Universities (C.I.A.U.) in 1967 and for Community Colleges (C.C.A.A.) in 1978.

CVA programs now receive support from Sport Canada and other affiliated bodies estimated at $750,000.00. These funds are mostly used for the high level programs of the Associations, such as the Men's and Women's National Teams, and elite players, coaches and officials programs. As National Sport Governing Body, it is also responsible of offering services to the Provincial/Territorial Associations in implementing their programs.

It is important to know that this structure is guided by representatives of each of these Regional Associations, members of the Board of Directors. To enhance this principle of representation, votes are awarded to each region according to membership. The Board of Directors meets twice every year and periodically elects an Executive Committee to be responsible for CVA's activities during the year. To involve the appropriate expertise, CVA has established committees, responsible for specific aspects of its programs. The Organizational Chart (1985) on the following page will give you a better image of CVA's structure (Chart 2).

REGIONAL ASSOCIATIONS

All Provinces and Territories of Canada have a structured association. The structure of each of them may differ, but responsibility is always given to a Board of Administrators elected by the members. Their objectives could be stated as:

- Promoting volleyball in their region
- Offering services for recreation, initiation and competition up to a national level

This will be reflected in the organization of provincial leagues and championships, support of provincial elite teams and of certification programs for officials and coaches, in the first three (3) levels of certification.

Your regional association probably offers other services of interest for your team or players. If you are not already involved, here is where you can contact your association:

REGIONAL ASSOCIATIONS

Newfoundland & Labrador Volleyball Assoc.
P.O. Box 9718
St. John's, NF
A1A 4J7

Manitoba Volleyball Association
1700 Ellice Avenue
Winnipeg, Manitoba
R3H 0B1

P.E.I. Volleyball Association
C/O Sport P.E.I.
Box 302
Charlottetown, P.E.I.
C1A 7K7

Saskatchewan Volleyball Association
1870 Lorne Street
Regina, Saskatchewan
S4P 2L7

Volleyball Nova Scotia
5516 Spring Garden Road
Halifax, N.S.
B3J 1G6

Alberta Volleyball Association
13 Mission Avenue
St. Albert, Alberta
T8N 1H6

Volleyball New Brunswick
Comp. 61, Site 9, S.S. 3
Fredericton, N.B.
E3B 5W9

B.C. Volleyball Association
1200 Hornby Street
Vancouver, B.C.
V6Z 2E2

Federation de Volleyball du Quebec
4545 Av. Pierre de Coubertin
C.P. 1000, Succ. M
Montreal, Quebec
HIV 3R2

N.W.T. Volleyball Association
Box 816
Yellowknife, N.W.T.
X1A 2N6

Ontario Volleyball Association
1220 Sheppard Avenue East
Willowdale, Ontario
M2K 2X1

Yukon Volleyball Association
Box 4972
Whitehorse, Yukon Territories
Y1A 4S2

Chart 2: CVA ORGANIZATIONAL CHART

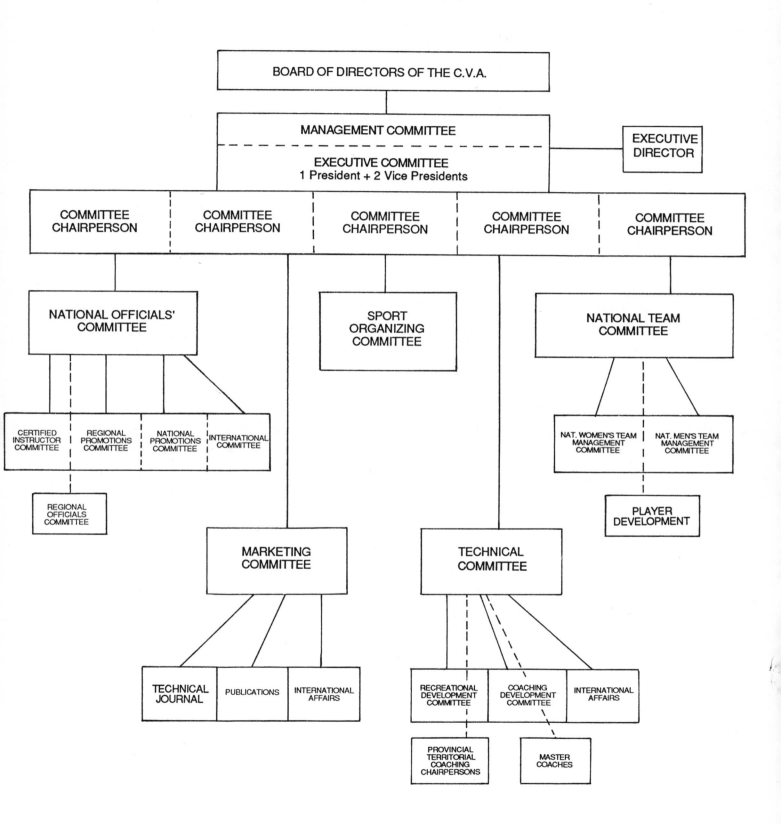

SUMMARY

- Most services offered to coaches and teams come directly from the Regional Associations.

- The Regional Associations represent each of the Provinces or Territories of Canada.

- Regional Associations are responsible for volleyball activities from initiation to national exposure.

- The Canadian Volleyball Association offers services to the Regional Associations and supports high performance programs such as the Men's and Women's National Teams.

- The CVA is a member of NORCECA, one of the five zones in the International Volleyball Federation (FIVB).